A New

Shakespearean

Poem?

A modern annotated text and transcription
of "The Paine of Pleasure" (1580)
attributed to
Edward de Vere, Earl of Oxford

Edited and with an introduction by Sarah Smith

max light books

Also by Sarah Smith

Chasing Shakespeares

The Vanished Child
The Knowledge of Water
A Citizen of the Country
Crimes and Survivors
The Other Side of Dark

For more about the poem
and to contact her, visit:
https://www.sarahsmith.com
Facebook sarahwriter, SarahSmithBooks
Twitter sarahwriter
Instagram swrs

for Bob Wyatt
Christopher Schelling
Rosemary Ahern
(and of course Ripley, Rio, Wiley, Radar, Otis, and Gunther)

omnia mei dona Dei

Contents

ABOUT THE EDITOR

Sarah Smith received her Ph.D. in English literature from Harvard, where she was a Graduate Prize Fellow in English and a Frank Knox Fellow; an article based on her thesis won Harvard's Bowdoin Prize. At Harvard, she studied Shakespeare under William Alfred, Harry Levin, Northrop Frye, and Robert Lowell. She has also received a Fulbright Fellowship and a Mellon Fellowship. After teaching at Northeastern, Tufts, and Boston University, she left the academic world for industry and writing.

She is the bestselling author of six novels: *The Vanished Child* (*New York Times* Notable Book; Waterstone's Book of the Year), *The Knowledge of Water* (*New York Times* Notable Book), *A Citizen of the Country*, *Chasing Shakespeares*, which Samuel Delany has called "the best novel about the Bard since *Nothing like the Sun*," *The Other Side of Dark*, which won both the Agatha and the Massachusetts Book Award, and *Crimes and Survivors.* Her work is published in fifteen languages.

She is also the author of two academic books and several academic articles, including one based on her discovery of Christina Rossetti's copy of Dante. She is the editor of *Total Amnesia*, the text and programming notes of Thomas Disch's *Amnesia*.

Contact her through www.sarahsmith.com .

ABOUT THE DESIGN

The eBook version of this book was coded using calibre; thanks to Kovid Goyal and the calibre team. The fonts used are Cambria, Old English Text MT, Trajan-Normal, and HamletOrNot.

The cover incorporates the following images, used under Creative Commons licenses:

- joewcampbell, http://www.flickr.com/photos/joewcampbell/3211616890/lightbox/
- Marcin Nowak ("London"), marcin-nowak-iXqTqC-f6jI-unsplash
- Sarah Smith, photograph of the first page of "The Paine of Pleasure"

The text is from the 1580 printing of *The Paine of Pleasure*.

The photograph of Sarah Smith is by Fred Perry.

INTRODUCTION

Mystery writer finds Shakespeare poem. Oh, right...

Once upon a time I taught English in colleges; now I write mysteries. A few years ago, I was doing a publicity tour in England for one of my books, *The Knowledge of Water,* which had just been published there. At the time I was working on what I expected to be a pleasant little comedy-mystery about why people believe the strange things they believe. Since I used to be an English professor, the mystery would be about the particular variant of Area 51 that most enrages English departments: whether William Shakespeare actually wrote the plays.

You may have heard something about the Shakespeare authorship. The story goes, William Shakespeare was Queen Elizabeth, or Christopher Marlowe, or Ben Jonson or the Earl of Derby. He was Mary Sidney, or even Cervantes. He was anyone but our familiar 1564-1616 of Stratford.

The story has been circulating for over two hundred years now. Otherwise quite sensible people give credence to it. Sigmund Freud. Walt Whitman. Henry James. Sir Derek Jacobi. Mark Rylance. Roland Emmerich made a movie of it.

I thought it was pretty much nonsense, but I wanted to know how the story had got into their heads. Like Jim Shapiro in *Contested Will,* I wanted to know why people believe what they believe.

I believe in Shakespeare; who doesn't believe in the man who wrote the plays? Joe Roper, the hero of my proposed comedy, believes in Shakespeare too. Like most believers, he has a personal stake. Joe was raised in a bankrupt small town, more or less like Stratford-on-Avon (which was going bankrupt when Shakespeare was a young man there). Joe's trying to escape East Bradenton, Vermont, and treasures a Shakespeare who managed to escape from *his* small town.

But at the beginning of the book, Joe finds a letter supposedly from William Shakespeare, saying he didn't write the plays. Joe wants to prove it's a forgery. Unfortunately, a Harvard graduate student, the rich and bratty Posy Gould, has seen the letter too, and is all ready to believe it and send it to the *Times*. "I'll give you a week to prove it's a forgery," Posy tells Joe, and they go to England to investigate.

I was at the point where Joe visits the British Library to dig into the connection between Shakespeare and an Elizabethan hack writer, Anthony Munday. I had about three days free in London, so of course I went to the British Library too.

The British Library is a reader's dream. Floors upon floors of lovely quiet reading rooms, where you can spend all day with books that you can't find anywhere else. People *bring* you books. Heaven. And what books! Lenin once said that the British Library had a better collection of books of Russian history than either Moscow or St. Petersburg. Every book that is published in Great Britain is theoretically there.

And, among other things, it has the largest extant collection of original editions of Anthony Munday's prose and poetry, an opportunity not to be missed.

Why Munday?

My hero Joe wants to find the Holy Grail of Shakespeare studies—the thing that will get him out of East Bradenton for sure, the thing an incautious person might assert that the poem you're about to read may be. The Holy Grail is any piece of Shakespeare's early work, the stuff he wrote before he was famous (and perhaps before he was entirely good). Not only would the Holy Grail show Shakespeare's genius developing, it might provide clues to how it developed, who he learned from, where he came from as a writer.

And Anthony Munday is associated with the most convincing of all those possible early works, *Sir Thomas More.*

It's not impossible to find new Shakespeare work. There has always been a merry trade in Shakespeare apocrypha. We've had at least two modern candidates, *A Funerall Elegye in memory of the late Vertuous Maister William Peeter*, and the lyric, "Shall I die?"—both of them, like most Shakespeare apocrypha, now attributed to someone else. But *Sir Thomas More* has never been entirely exploded.

The manuscript of *More,* now among the great treasures of

the British Library, is a grubby little thing, a few long handwritten pages. Anthony Munday supposedly wrote most of it—the manuscript has changes in his hand, which look like author's changes—but there are also bits in other handwritings. One of them, one rather crabbed Elizabethan hand, "Hand D," has added an entire scene. And this, the "Ill May Day" scene, may be the one piece of manuscript writing we have by Shakespeare. Rush off and read the scene now.[1] Here's a little of it, part of an eloquent defense of what Shakespeare would call "degree":

> ...What do you then
> Rising 'gainst him that God himself installs
> But rise 'gainst God? What do you to your souls
> In doing this?

More dates from 1596 or earlier, perhaps as early as 1590, perhaps even earlier than that. In comparison with most of what was being written in England then, the "Ill May Day" scene is very, very good. It is written in blank verse, not rhymed. The verse is irregularly stressed, not the ta-*dum*-ta-*dum* "rocker verse" that was in fashion in the period. Rather than coming to a stop at the end of each line, the lines run on: "What do you to your souls in doing this?" And it shows a true dramatic voice, the voice of an actual breathing person—unlike most of its fellow apocrypha, it's good enough to be Shakespeare.

Based on the similarity of the handwriting to Shakespeare's, based on the quality of the verse and on other similarities between the scene and Shakespeare's work, the Ill May Day scene has been asserted to be Shakespeare's.[2]

But there's a rather odd thing about *Sir Thomas More*. Read the rest of the play. You'll find other speeches that show the same characteristics, the same eloquence—but in Munday's handwriting. Here's Lady More's soliloquy from late in the play:

> Me thought 'twas night,
> And that the king and queen went on the Thames
> In barges to hear music: my lord and I
> Were in a little boat...and, being near,

We grappled to the barge that bare the king.
But after many pleasing voices spent
In that still moving music house, me thought
The violence of the stream did sever us
Quite from the golden fleet, and hurried us
Unto the bridge, which with unusèd horror
We entered at full tide; our boat stood still
Just opposite the Tower, and there it turned
And turned about, as when a whirl-pool sucks
The circled waters; me thought that we both cried
Till that we sunk; when arm in arm we died.

Blank verse, irregular scansion, run-on lines, and a fine dramatic voice: This sounds rather Shakespearean too. Was Anthony Munday actually a writer who could be compared with early Shakespeare?

Or, could it be possible, did Shakespeare have more to do with *Sir Thomas More* than anyone has realized?

Might...in fact...might *Sir Thomas More* be in some part an early and undiscovered Shakespeare play?

That's what my hero Joe thinks. Joe wants to find out that Shakespeare wrote those other scenes in *Sir Thomas More.* And if he had, if Shakespeare worked with Munday, did he know Munday? Were they friends or writing partners? Did Shakespeare and Munday ever do anything together again?

And if Shakespeare and Munday collaborated again, *can Joe find what they wrote?*

That would make folks sit up and take notice, Joe thinks. So he sits down to read all of Munday, all fifty or so volumes.

So did I.

Unless he wrote *More,* Munday was not an outstanding writer even in his own day. Four hundred years later, he's heavy going. I found the poem described here about midday on the last day I could devote to research, before going to York for a conference. It was bound together with a couple of other books I'd got out to read; it had no title page and the date scribbled on the first page was early, 1585. The title was far from promising: "The Paine of Pleasure." H'm.

I handed it in unread, then gave way to twinges of conscience and asked for it back.

Within a few minutes it was clear that this was a different sort of poem, and rather more attractive, than what I'd been reading. I didn't think it was Munday's. (Later I would find out that Munday's authorship has been questioned since the nineteenth century.) But whose was it? I didn't have time to investigate; I'd probably never find another copy of the poem; but the wonderful staff of the British Library agreed to Xerox it for me.

Off to York and the delights of being on a panel with Ruth Rendell, but in weather as bad as I'd ever experienced in England. It was raining; it was flooding. (For some reason, the publication of *The Knowledge of Water* has been followed by disastrous floods in both America and Britain. I blame myself.) By the time I got back, just in time to pick up my Xerox and head to the airport, the wind was a full-bore hurricane. At Heathrow, our plane prepared to take off into 90mph headwinds. We were taxi-ing down the runway, the 747 jumping about like spit on a griddle.

To console myself for my imminent death, I started reading the poem. What a nice line—how well he says that—what a well-chosen word—what a *rare* word, perhaps he has made it up? It was a poem of the 1580s, to be sure, and few poems of that period are entirely attractive even to scholars; but it was one of those little golden moments that make research worthwhile.

And it sounded like— Probably it sounded like nothing but my imagination; after all, I was writing a book about people on the track of Shakespeare. Still, I clasped my hands and prayed: "Don't let me die, don't let me die, I have to tell someone about this."

We landed. I was too strung to go to sleep. At 4 AM the next morning, I was sitting in bed surrounded by the *Oxford English Dictionary*, checking words, delighted by how nicely he had used them. 1585...it could be an early Shakespeare poem. A *very* early Shakespeare poem. In 1585, he was only 21...

At that point I had nothing for a date but a handwritten suggestion on the first page. The British Library copy doesn't have a title page. But the other, in the Cambridge University Library, did, so I wrote to a friend in London and asked her to find and Xerox the Cambridge title page, to check the date there.

I believed in Shakespeare. (I still believe in Shakespeare; who doesn't believe in the man who wrote the plays?) But I believed in the poem too.

And Joe and I were about to get a rather nasty shock. Because the title page said 1580.

17. October. 1580;

Too early for Shakespeare; at least, too early for William Shakespeare, 1564-1616.

Joe had, more or less, a nervous breakdown. I rewrote the book.

I'm a mystery writer. And I had a mystery to solve. If this wasn't Shakespeare's poem, who could be so interestingly good, in such a Shakespearean way? As far back as 1580, back with the dinosaurs?

Why hadn't anyone heard of him before?

Could I find out anything more about the man who had written it?

That's what this essay is about. Read the essay, which is more formal than this introduction and has lots of footnotes, but is a pretty good mystery story.

Read the poem. See what you think.

If you're interested, get in touch with me through www.sarahsmith.com, or on Facebook as sarahwriter.

You could be about to read a new Shakespeare poem.

Take a deep breath.

Enjoy.

A NEW SHAKESPEAREAN POEM?

In my novel *Chasing Shakespeares,*[3] an ardent Shakespearean scholar comes across a long poem, "The Paine of Pleasure," traditionally ascribed to Anthony Munday. My hero decides the poem cannot possibly be by Munday; it is by an upper-class poet; and it sounds Shakespearean—which bothers him deeply.

The purpose of this essay is to discuss this attribution and the "Shakespearean" qualities of the poem in more detail.

From internal evidence, the poem was not written by Munday or the other person to whom it has been attributed, Nicholas Breton; it is unlike their contemporary work in style and scope. Again from internal evidence, "The Paine of Pleasure" was probably written by a poet familiar with the court. In his *Elizabethan Courtier Poets,* Steven May has identified about forty such poets, and of those, the most likely candidate is Edward de Vere, seventeenth Earl of Oxford, who was Munday's employer at the time "The Paine of Pleasure" was published.

I believe it to be a previously unidentified poem by Edward de Vere, Earl of Oxford. At this writing, Steven May, editor of Oxford's poetry, and Alan Nelson, one of Oxford's biographers, see no reason to doubt "The Paine of Pleasure" is Oxford's, though neither of them agrees with my other conclusions.

We will not be dealing with a major undiscovered

Shakespearean work; in many ways "The Paine of Pleasure" is a fairly typical late mid-century poem. Like *More*, it may have been written by more than one person. However, the poem is important, for no other reason, because of its size (1200 lines, 36 printed pages), its early date, and its poetic characteristics, which are unlike almost any other poem of the period. These characteristics include irregular rhythm, the use of nonce words and metaphors taken from sports, run-on lines, secularism, a drawing away from allegory and the morality-play tradition, and the use of dramatic voices.

The same characteristics are also distinctive to the work of William Shakespeare. Seeing "Shakespearean" characteristics so early, and in a context where William Shakespeare of Stratford is unlikely to have produced them, leads to one of two conclusions.

It is possible that more authors wrote like Shakespeare in the late 1570s than we have previously recognized. A full discussion of the poetic practice of the late 1570s is outside the scope of this paper, but we will look at a few other poets writing in London in the period. Most do not write like Shakespeare, or even like this poet.

If a poem written before October 1580 does have significant and otherwise inexplicable similarities to Shakespeare's work, it is important, not only for itself, but in its implications for further research. We may have been looking for Shakespeare's early work in the wrong times and places, and there may be more to find. I'll talk about some potential research areas at the end of this essay.

BIBLIOGRAPHICAL DESCRIPTION OF "THE PAINE OF PLEASURE"

The first appearance of *a* book called *The Paine of Pleasure* is in a *Stationer's Registry* entry for September 9, 1578; it is described as a compilation by Nicholas Breton, licensed to Richard or Rhys Jones.[4] It is unclear what relationship that book has to *The Paine of Pleasure* as we know it, since from the evidence of the single surviving title page, *The Paine of Pleasure* was printed not for Jones but for Henry Carr by an unnamed printer, who I believe was

John Charlewood[5], and was published on October 17, 1580. This unique perfect copy survives in the Pepysian Library in Cambridge (Pepysian Library, no. 1434; ESTC S94255). Besides the two poems, it includes the title page, two short dedications (one to the notorious Lady Douglas Sheffield, one to the reader), and "Amorous Epistles," a sixteen-page selection of letters and riddles in prose and verse.[6]

The second copy, now in the British Library (C.57.d.49.(3.); ESTC S126004), comprises only the two long poems, "The Paine of Pleasure" and "The Author's Dream." This fragment is bound up in a single volume with copies of *The Paradise of Dainty Devices* and *The Gorgeous Gallery of Gallant Inventions*; this volume once belonged to the antiquarian Anthony à Wood, who has annotated *The Paradise of Dainty Devices* with the information that the "E.O." poems in this volume were by the Earl of Oxford, and noted on the first page of "The Paine of Pleasure" that the author was Munday and the publication date was 1585.

These two copies have sometimes been taken to represent two editions; however, the two texts of the poem are identical. It is almost certain that these two books represent two copies of a single printing.

The Paine of Pleasure has been reprinted by UMI (Ann Arbor MI, 1988) as Early English Books, Tract Supplement D33 (C.57.D.49[3]); this reprint apparently contains only the two poems. The poem has had a modern reprint on Literature Online, where it is ascribed to Munday and given the date 1583. The book is not yet reproduced in Early English Books Online.

CONTENT, STYLE, AND SUBJECT

In many ways, including the quality of much of the verse, "The Paine of Pleasure" is a representative mid-century *vanitas vanitatum* poem: Vanity, vanity, all is vanity, and every joy is but a toy. The poem is written in ABABCC rhyme and iambic pentameter—the "Venus and Adonis" pattern and meter, common in English poetry of the period. It is divided into an introduction and 23 chapters, ranging from one stanza to several pages in length; and, in a thoroughgoing case of *amplificatio*—repeating the moral until it is pounded into the reader's head—every chapter but the last argues that worldly pleasures yield nothing but pain.

It is more accurate, however, to say that the *ostensible* subject of "The Paine of Pleasure" is the vanity of worldly pleasure. Much of the energy of the poem goes instead to the descriptions of secular pleasures and the vigorous portraits of disappointment. The usual thrust of a mid-century vanities poem is toward abstraction and didacticism, but the thrust of "The Paine of Pleasure" is secular, concrete, and unusually interested in the psychology of self-indulgence.

What gives this poet pleasure? After the first abstractions (beauty, riches, honor, love), the poet's toys are a surprisingly specific mix of sports and learning. His sports are riding and horse-training, hawks, dogs, music, dancing, wrestling, climbing, fencing, tennis, archery, bowling, fishing, and fowling. He studies physic, law, astronomy, physiognomy, cosmography, philosophy, arithmetic, logic, rhetoric, and the only lasting pleasure, divinity.

The author of "The Paine of Pleasure" paints attractive pictures of these toys:

> What sport it is to see an arrow fly,
> A gallant archer cleanly draw his bow,
> In shooting off, again how cunningly
> He hath his loose, in letting of it go:
> To nock it sure, and draw it to the head
> And then fly out, hold straight, and strike it dead...[7]

But pleasures bring dangers. In "The Paine of Pleasure" climbers fall, horses and dancers go lame, and hawks escape; those who play with toys play with fire.

> Perhaps again, you have your eye thrust out,
> Or catch a scratch cross overthwart your face:
> Or else be swaddled roughly round about,
> Both shoulders, sides, arms, legs, and every place.
> At parting now, Sir, when you feel the smart
> Will you not think Fencing a joyful Art?
> ("Fencing")

The psychological and moral dangers of pleasure are as great as the physical ones. The archer ruins himself for pleasure:

> But that one shot is e'en enough to make
> Him sell his coat for store of bow and shafts,
> The cost whereof will make his heart to ache...
> ("Shooting")

The man who has found riches becomes a miser:

> In Riches now, another kind of joy,
> In which both youth and age have great delight:
> Were it well weighed, and it were but a toy,
> Which many ways do breed their great despite.
> In getting first with labour, care and pain,
> In keeping too, as great unrest again.
> ("Riches")

Beauty destroys the beautiful:

> Beautie in some doth cause a kind of pride,
> And pride must be maintained all by cost...
> ("Beauty")

The author of "The Paine of Pleasure" is more interested in psychology than sin. He makes very little distinction between Hell and the hell in the mind; the pains of pleasure are very close to the pains of life itself. He is not interested in abstract characters; his abstractions turn instead into extended Lyly-like metaphors, feathers in a mental tempest:

> And for the joys that in our life we find,
> Which are but few, and yet not free from woe,
> What are they all, but feathers in the wind
> Which every tempest tosseth to and fro,
> Which tempests so, are rising every day
> As in short space blow all our joys away.

([Introduction])

The poet balances delight and remorse, pleasure and a rueful knowledge of its cost. (The cost of pleasure is a frequent theme.) In general the seesawing is too fast to give the poet time for a sustained effect, but the poetic immaturity is combined with unusual psychological acumen and complexity.

INTERNAL CLUES ABOUT THE AUTHOR

The poetic voice of "The Paine of Pleasure" is that of a man from the privileged classes. The poet refers offhandedly to buying jewels, using law to keep "one's own," and having a choice between training one's own horse and having it trained for one.

> What gem so rare may please their mistress's eye
> Cost lands and life, but Lovers daily buy.
> ("Love")

> Nowe he again that never takes the pain
> To break [a horse] so, but have him broke to hand,
> I think indeed hath more joy of the twain...
> ("Horses, Hawks, and Hounds")

The author speaks authoritatively about training hawks, singing and dancing, fencing, playing tennis, shooting at archery, bowling, and listening to courtly music—all upper-class pursuits— as well as acquiring what seems to be a comprehensive course of Renaissance studies.

> Some love to see the goshawk roughly rush
> Thorough the woods, and perch from tree to tree
> And seize upon the pheasant in the bush,
> And sure it is a pretty sport to see...
> ("Horses, Hawks, and Hounds")

What sport is it to cut a Ball in kind
Or strike a Ball into the hazard fine,
Or bandy balls to fly against the wind
Or strike a ball low, level o'er the line,
Or make a chase or hazard for a game,
Then with a brickle wall to winne the same.
("Tennis")

These casual references to upper-class concerns and circumstances (owning at least one horse, owning musical instruments, listening to courtly music, playing bowling and tennis, and reading extensively) suggest that the author came from the upper classes or had equivalent leisure and money.

USE OF RHYTHM, ADVANCED FOR THE PERIOD

Perhaps the greatest pleasure of the poem is its remarkably advanced use of poetic rhythm. Rhythm serves sense; rhythm is witty and varied.

Minims, Crochets, Quavers, Sharps, Flats, to fain:
Ut, re, me, fa, sol, la, and back again.
("Music")

Rhythm even successfully mimics the cadence of the ordinary speaking voice—here, an Elizabethan fencing-master and some bystanders at an archery match:

Lie here, lie there, strike out your blow at length,
Strike and thrust with him, look to your dagger hand:
Believe me, Sir, you bear a gallant strength...
("Fencing")

"Tush," says another, "he may be excused,
Since the last mark, the wind doth greater grow."
At last he claps in the white suddenly,

Then "Oh, well shot!" the standers by do cry.
{("Shooting")

The poet uses large numbers of irregular stresses and half-stresses. He has a showman's sense of rhythm, and rhythm is gracefully married to meaning. The highly irregular line "At last he claps in the white suddenly," with its two strong successive stresses, "*white sud*denly," begs to be read with a little pause at the moment when the novice archer stops dead and realizes he has actually hit the target. "*Ut, re, me, fa, sol, la,* and back again," almost a whole line of half-stresses, glides like a singer's voice up the scale. Regular lines describing vanities are followed by one beautiful and extremely irregular line that escapes both vanity and its rhythm:

Divinity doth number out our days,
And shows our life, still fading as a flower,
Bids us beware of wanton wicked ways,
For we are sure to live no certain hour.
Arithmetic doth number worldly toys,
Divinity innumerable joys.
("Divinity")

INTERNAL CLUES ABOUT THE COMPOSITION

From internal evidence, "The Paine of Pleasure" seems to have been tossed off very quickly. Music is written about twice; the pleasures of hounds are promised but not performed, and astronomy and cosmography are barely glanced at. The poem was not extensively copyedited before printing and several lines are garbled. It may have been set from a manuscript in secretary hand, since one apparent misprint ("stands upon no ground" for "stamps upon the ground") would have been easy to make in secretary hand.

It is possible that the poem was written by two men. If so, one was more interested in the subject of repentance, the other in the subject of pleasure. The first writer-voice is moralistic; every joy is but a childish toy. The second voice silently subverts the moralistic tags. Instead of repeating the joy-toy rhyme, he rings changes on it. Instead of lamenting the pleasurable world, he ruefully celebrates it and mourns it. The quality of the verse changes drastically as well, from rocker verse to something far more rhythmically daring.

WHO WROTE "THE PAINE OF PLEASURE"?

The most obvious candidates are Nicholas Breton, to whom the compilation is attributed in the 1578 *SR* entry, and Anthony Munday, whose name is on the compilation.

NICHOLAS BRETON

Stylistically, "The Paine of Pleasure" might in part be Breton's; it resembles some of his work in *The Works of a Young Wit* and *A Flourish upon Fancy,* especially a poem on dancing in the former collection. Like the author of "The Paine of Pleasure," Breton writes multiple linked poems. He frequently uses the poem's ABABCC rhyme scheme or the iambic hexameter of "The Author's Dream," the other major poem in the collection.

In addition, as we shall see, "The Paine of Pleasure" seems to have thematic similarities to "The Grief of Joy," the last major poem of the well-known Elizabethan poet George Gascoigne. Breton was Gascoigne's stepson; he would have had access to this work, which was unpublished and largely unavailable in 1580.

Other parts of the compilation have been attributed to Breton. The "Amorous Epistles," letters in mixed prose and poetry included in *The Paine of Pleasure,* are catalogued by Harvard as by him. Breton was the author of *A Post with a Packet of Mad Letters,* and this is a reasonable attribution of that part of the book.[8] Breton wrote poems resembling "The Author's Dream," and that poem may be his.[9]

However, Breton's voice as a poet is strikingly unlike that of the author of "The Paine of Pleasure." At this period, Breton almost invariably writes in the voice of a young literary man showing off his talent, the "young wit" of the *Works of a Young Wit.* He does not use rare or unusual words or metaphors from sport; indeed, he uses few metaphors at all. He writes rocker verse, the regularly stressed verse popular in the mid-century, rather than experimenting with rhythm. He does not write about specifics or psychology; the typical Breton poem talks about "a lady" and "a gentleman," abstract as Jell-O, in "a garden" where allegory and a moral lurk just under the enameled mid-century surface. Breton describes himself as a gentleman, but he does not live in the leisured circumstances the author of "The Paine of Pleasure" so easily assumes.

Most telling, Breton has no interest whatsoever in the tangled psychology of pleasure and pain. The poem by Breton that is most like "The Paine of Pleasure" is introduced as "A pretty passion, penned in the behalf of a gentleman who, traveling into Kent, fell there in love; and venturing both lands, limb, and life, to do his Mistress's service, in long time reaped nothing but loss for his labor." The first few lines promise well for Breton's authorship of "The Paine of Pleasure":

> When I sometime revolve within my mind
> The sorrows strange that some men seem to show
> And therewithal consider eke in kind
> The causes first, whereof their griefs do grow
> And then compare, their pains with mine again,
> I find them all but pleasures to my pain...[10]

But within several stanzas the poet has become a standard heartsick swain, who languishes generically on for several pages:

> Why am I sick? Yea sure, I am not well
> Where lies my grief, in body or in mind,
> In both, God wot, which more I cannot tell,
> And I am sure physician none to find
> That can devise to cure my strange disease
> Save God and you, who may when so you please.[11]

It is not impossible that Breton wrote some part of "The Paine of Pleasure," especially since he may have been originally the editor or compiler of the volume it appeared in. But what makes "The Paine of Pleasure" most interesting is what makes it least like Breton's work.

ANTHONY MUNDAY

Anthony Munday may also have written some part of "The Paine of Pleasure." However, like Breton, his voice does not match what makes "The Paine of Pleasure" interesting.

Externally, the evidence for Munday's authorship comes from two sources. The first is Anthony à Wood's annotation of the imperfect copy now in the British Library: Wood says that the author is Munday. However, Wood is writing a century after the fact and he is wrong about the date of the book; there is no reason to consider his evidence more than hearsay.

The second is the evidence of the complete copy in the Pepysian Library. In this copy, Munday's name is on the dedications but only his motto on the title page. This is strong evidence that Munday was the compiler of the book, but not that he was the author of all the material in it. Anthologizers, translators, or even printers commonly signed dedications; it is not a reliable proof of authorship. Since Munday was known to be doing anthologies and/or contributing prefaces and/or poems to them during this period, we may reasonably conclude that he could have been the compiler of *The Paine of Pleasure*, without needing to infer that he wrote the title poem.[12]

Comparing Munday's style, content, and use of rhythm in his collection of poems *The Mirror of Mutabilitie,* published the previous year, suggests even more strongly that he did not write "The Paine of Pleasure."

Like "The Paine of Pleasure," the *Mutability* poems are didactic poems in ABABCC rhyme. Beyond that, they are dissimilar. The *Mutability* poems get all their energy from didacticism.

> Think not to live as Gods upon the land,
> Remember still that Pride will have a fall:
> Consider you are Subject to God's hand,
> And in a moment pass away you shall.
> Live still to die, that you may ready be:
> When God shall call each one in his degree.
>
> See how my Pride was quickly laid in dust,
> Behold you may my Mutability:

> My Princely rule wheron I whole did trust,
> Did naught avail my state to fortify.
> He set me up, again, he brought me low:
> That I to you a warning plain might show.[13]

Munday is expert at bringing abstractions such as Pride and Avarice to dire life, and is comfortable with the limitations of character portrayal and psychology it imposes.

Approach to rhythmic style also differentiates Munday from the author of "The Paine of Pleasure." Like Breton, Munday writes rocker verse. Writing regularly stressed verse was a skill much admired at the time, and Munday is dreadfully good at it. However, unlike the "Paine" poet, given a choice between meter and sense, he is inclined to choose meter.

> O seely Samson now deprived of joy,
> Where is the life that thou didst lead of yore?
> Is comfort turn'd to direfull dark annoy,
> Is all thy fame now dead thou hadst before?
> Why? is it thou that burnt thy enemy's Corn?
> Behold thy self (alas) thou art forlorn.
> (*Mut.*, "Samson")

Munday's rhythmic practice fits comfortably into the midcentury, while that of "The Paine of Pleasure" looks forward to the end of the century.

Finally, Munday's social assumptions are different than those of the poet of "The Paine of Pleasure." Munday, for example, refers offhandedly to working for wages:

> They traitor-like mine eyes pulled from my head,
> And in the mill did use me like a slave:
> Behold my wife what courtesy she bred,
> See for my love what recompense I have.
> Now grind poor wretch thy living for to get:
> To find thee clothes, and also bread and meat.
> (*Mut.*, "Samson")

In summary, the style of "The Paine of Pleasure" does not resemble Munday's in the near-contemporaneous *Mutability* poems. The experience described and implied in "Paine" seems to be that of a writer of the upper classes. Though Munday was secretary to an earl, from the evidence of the *Mutability* poems he does not write about upper-class experience in the same natural way as does the poet of "The Paine of Pleasure". The traditional attribution of the poem to Munday does not rest on any strong external evidence and has been previously questioned.

It is possible that Munday wrote part of the poem. But if so, he probably collaborated with another poet.

THE CASE FOR AN AUTHOR FAMILIAR WITH THE COURT

Internal and external evidence suggests that the other poet was not only upper- class, but frequented the court.

Not all men who were at court (and the court was mostly male) were courtiers. Steven May defines a courtier as someone who was allowed access not only to the semi-public Presence Chamber but to Queen Elizabeth's Privy Chamber—Elizabeth's suite of private apartments, where only her closest friends and favorites could go. Nothing in the poem allows us to restrict the identity of the poet that closely; however, we are most likely to find our mystery poet, if he can be found, by looking in the courtier poets May identifies, in tandem with other poets known to have frequented the court.

May defines a courtier poet by the following:

- Courtier poets exchanged gifts with Queen Elizabeth at New Year's.
- They received from the crown lodgings, food, and candle allowance ("chambers, diet, and bouge of court").
- Elizabeth gave them or their children wedding or christening gifts.
- They had rewards or patronage from the crown.
- The male courtier poets participated in court tournaments.

There are no references to wedding or christening gifts in

"The Paine of Pleasure." However, the other four parts of the definition are at least hinted at. The author refers to courtiers' "climbing" for patronage several times in the poem. He casually mentions one of Elizabeth's castles, Hertford, in a way that suggests a court in-joke:

> Why, if there be some such odd fiddling Clown
> As plays at Hertford on the Holidays...
> ("Music")[14]

The material on training horses ("Horses, Hawks, and Hounds") shows that the author knows horses and is familiar with courtly sports such as hawking on horseback.

Finally, "The Paine of Pleasure" has a specific connection not only to Elizabeth's court but to court poetry. The most readily identifiable precursor to "The Paine of Pleasure" is a poem that would have been known almost exclusively by persons who were at court in the period 1577-1580.

THE POSSIBLE INFLUENCE OF GEORGE GASCOIGNE'S "THE GRIEF OF JOY"

The Elizabethan age produced many, many *vanitas vanitatum* poems; there is and will be no proof that the author of "The Paine of Pleasure" was specifically imitating any one of them. However, a near-contemporary poem, George Gascoigne's "The Grief of Joy," is strikingly similar in title, in content, and— most important for a poet—in rhythmic sophistication and voice.

George Gascoigne presented "The Grief of Joy," his last major work, to Queen Elizabeth on New Year's Day 1576/7.[15] It consists of a preface and four "songs", "The Griefs or Discommodities of Lusty Youth," "The Vanities of Beauty," "The Faults of Force and Strength," and "The Vanities of Activities."

The content of "The Grief of Joy" overlaps to a significant degree that of "The Paine of Pleasure." Both poets talk about beauty, riches, fencing, leaping, riding, and other activities, almost never seen together elsewhere in *vanitas* poetry. Both use (indeed overuse) the words *joy* and *toy*. One is in ABABCC mode; the preface to the other is. Both paint attractive, specific pictures of court life. The energy of both is secular, a vivid contemporary portraiture. Gascoigne may even have provided "The Paine of Pleasure" with its title; "no pleasure free from pain," he writes.[16]

"The Grief of Joy" has a subtlety of rhythmic effects and energy of diction that closely resemble those in "The Paine of Pleasure":

> The heavens on high perpetually do move
> By minutes meal the hour doth steal away
> By hours the day, by days the months remove
> And then by months the years as fast decay
> Yea, Virgil's verse and Tully's truth do say
> That time flies on and never claps her wings,
> But rides on clouds , and forward still she flings....
>
> What said I? days? nay, not so many hours
> Not hours? no no so many minutes not
> The bravest youth, which flourisheth like flowers,
> Would think his hue to be as soon forgot,
> As tender herbs cut up to serve the pot.
> And then this life, which he so thought to climb,
> Would show itself but tumbling under time...
>
> True joy cannot in trifling toys consist
> Nor happiness in joys which soon decay
> Then look on youth, and mark it, he that list,
> Sometimes both born and buried in a day
> Yea, though it should continue green alway,
> I cannot find what joy therein doth grow,
> Which is not stayed with undertwigs of woe.[17]

Gascoigne is a strong poet and there is a great deal to admire here: homely metaphors ("tender herbs cut up to serve the pot"), energetic abstraction ("time...rides on clouds, and forward still she flings"), varied rhythm, and above all a human speaking voice. "What said I? Days? Nay, not so many hours/Not hours? No no so many minutes not...."

Gascoigne was one of the leading poets of his time and "The Grief of Joy" is one of the best poems of his late period; one would think that the audiences who heard it at Elizabeth's court, or read it in manuscript, must have found it very good indeed. But the poem was apparently not popular. Gascoigne did not publish it before his death the following November, and it was not printed until Hazlitt's edition of the *Works* in 1868-70. It does not appear to have had wide circulation in manuscript.[18] For this reason, if the poet of "The Paine of Pleasure" was imitating "The Grief of Joy", he probably saw it in Gascoigne's papers, read the manuscript presented to Elizabeth, or heard it during a reading at court.

Thus the horse-owning, jewel-giving poet of "The Paine of Pleasure" may well be either one of Steven May's courtier poets or some other poet at court sometime between January 1577 and October 1580.[19] We cannot definitively identify him; but starting from May's list of less than forty poets and their biographical data, we can speculate who he might be.

MAY'S IDENTIFIED COURTIER POETS, AND OTHER POETS AT THE COURT

May lists thirty-two known courtier poets, plus non-courtiers known to have presented "courtly poetry" to Elizabeth or to have been resident at Court. Many of these can be knocked out of contention for one or more reasons:

- They are female. The poet speaks from male experience; Lady Elizabeth Cooke Hoby Russell and Lady Mary Sidney are unlikely candidates.
- They collected their poetry, which did not include this poem. Sir Walter Raleigh and Fulke Greville, Lord Brooke, for example, had leisure to edit their own literary works; if either wrote "The Paine of Pleasure," neither claimed it. Sir Arthur Gorges' poetry was collected in manuscript; if he wrote this substantial poem by his twenty-third year, it did not find its way into his collection.[20] Mary Sidney edited her brother Sir Philip Sidney's poetry and did not include "The Paine of Pleasure." Thomas Churchyard published his own poetry abundantly, and did not claim "The Paine of

Pleasure."

- Many of these poets, of course, can also be dismissed on stylistic grounds, e.g. John Lyly, George Puttenham, and George Peele.
- Some poets may be dismissed because all their known poetry is in another language, for example Petruccio Ubaldini (Italian) and Dr. Thomas Wilson and Sir John Wolley (Latin).
- Some poets must be dismissed simply because we have no or almost no specimens of their work. They *may* have written "The Paine of Pleasure," but if so, we will never know it. Among these poets are George Clifford, third Earl of Cumberland, Gilbert Talbot, seventh earl of Stanhope, Sir Walter Mildmay, and Sir Edward Hoby. Sir Thomas Heneage's longest known poem is less than twenty lines; though it is in ABABCC form and iambic pentameter, it is virtually impossible to compare with "The Paine of Pleasure," and he too must be considered at best a non-proven.
- For other poets, we have specimens, but in different genres or written at substantially different periods of their lives; thus we have nothing to compare this poem with directly. Of Sir Christopher Hatton we have only the fourth act of *Gismond of Salern* (ca. 1567), though he is known to have written verse to Elizabeth. The poems of Saint Philip Howard, Earl of Arundel, all date from after his conversion.[21] Sir Thomas Sackville's only identified extant poem is a verse epistle dated ca. 1566-1574. Sir John Harington's extant work is epigrams and translations; Sir Edward Dyer's nine surviving poems are love lyrics. On the evidence of their extant work, none of these men is the poet of "The Paine of Pleasure."

Biographical details eliminate some candidates:

- Since writing a substantial poem takes energy, it is unlikely the poet was an old man by 1580. Sir William Cordell (d. 1581) and Sir John Harington (d. 1582) are unlikely candidates.

- Since the poem describes a Renaissance education of a fairly modern sort, the poet is more likely to have been born in the 1540s or later than in the 1530s or earlier. Sir Henry Lee (b. 1533) and Thomas Sackville, Earl of Dorset (b. 1535) are not likely candidates; nor are Sir William Cecil[22] or Thomas Churchyard.

If the poet of "The Paine of Pleasure" imitated Gascoigne and wrote the poem between 1577 and 1580, we can infer additional biographical details about him:

- He must have been born by about 1560 since he must have been old enough to be at Court by 1579 at the latest, and preferably by 1577, and old enough to complete a substantial poem by 1580. Essex, born in 1565, is too young. Sir Robert Sidney, born in 1563, is known not to have attended Court until 1581.[23]
- He must have had leisure to compose a substantial poem after January 1577 and to approve, if not oversee, its publication in 1580. Sir Francis Drake and Henry Neel had embarked on Sir Humphrey Gilbert's voyage of exploration in 1578 and did not return until October 1580, the month of the poem's publication.
- He is likely to have had the reputation of writing substantial pieces, or substantial pieces of his must be known to have existed; "The Paine of Pleasure" was not the author's first work.

We have deduced that the author is likely to have been a male member of the upper classes, born by about 1560, with a good Renaissance education, interested in upper-class sports.[24] He may have been present at Court sometime between 1577 and 1580, and may have had access to manuscripts in the Queen's library or attended readings of Gascoigne's manuscript "The Grief of Joy". He had time and energy to compose a substantial poem before October 1580. By 1580 he had composed other literary work, which does not survive or is no longer identified as his.

There is one final piece of useful biographical information: the context in which the poem was published. There was, of course, no stricture against writing poetry—it was one of a gentleman's talents—and none against circulating it in manuscript or reading it aloud at court. Indeed, Elizabeth's court was known for reading aloud:

> ...the stranger that entereth into the court of England upon the sudden, shall rather imagine himself to come into some public school of the universities, where many give ear to one that readeth, than into a prince's palace...[25]

Nor, Steven May has argued, was there a stricture against publishing poetry. Lady Mary Sidney published her brother's poetry not long after his death. Fulke Greville published his own work.

But with *The Paine of Pleasure*, we are dealing with a rather special case. First, it is early. Sidney's poetry was published in 1591, Greville's not until the seventeenth century. Second, it was not published alone as a showcase for the author's individual work, as were Sidney's and Greville's poems. The other participants in *The Paine of Pleasure*, apart from our hypothetical court poet, were the bourgeois Anthony Munday and possibly Nicholas Breton.

In the period around 1580, only two of May's courtier poets are known to have appeared in a collection with bourgeois authors.[26] One is Thomas, Lord Vaux, some of whose poems appeared in *The Paradise of Dainty Devices* in 1576. However, he can hardly be said to have participated enthusiastically, since he had died in 1556 (thus certainly could not have written "The Paine of Pleasure" after 1577).

The only living courtier poet who is known to have allowed his poems to appear in a collection with bourgeois authors before 1580 is also the only one of May's courtier poets whom we cannot eliminate on other grounds as the poet of "The Paine of Pleasure."

Of May's listing of court poets—based on his examination of over 32,000 printed and manuscript Elizabethan poems—the man who is most likely to have written "The Paine of Pleasure" is the man whose early poetry appeared with Vaux's in *Paradise:* Edward de Vere, Earl of Oxford.

In 1580, of course, Oxford was also Munday's employer.

THE BIOGRAPHICAL CASE FOR OXFORD

Nothing in Oxford's life or work is inconsistent with his having written "The Paine of Pleasure."

In May's sense, he qualifies easily as a courtier; he was the seventeenth earl of Oxford, hereditary Lord Great Chamberlain, and, after the Duke of Norfolk's beheading in 1572, the senior nobleman of England. He exchanged gifts with Elizabeth, was frequently at her court between 1577 and 1580, received wedding and christening gifts from her, participated in court tournaments, and requested and received patronage from the crown.

Oxford's biographical data is also consistent with everything the poet says or implies about himself. These details are not smoking guns—many Elizabethan gallants lived on the fine edge of financial ruin, grew despondent, knew how to sing and dance, and had studied the law and astronomy—but they do not argue against him.

Summarizing the biographical data:

- Age: Born in 1550, Oxford was both old enough and young enough to have written the poem.
- Presence at Court: As a ward of Elizabeth's private secretary, Sir William Cecil, Oxford had attended court regularly since 1562.
- Acquaintance with Queen Elizabeth: Oxford was one of Elizabeth's favorites, close enough to have his own nickname, her "Turk."
- Vanity of all earthly things: At the time the poem was published, Oxford had ample reason to consider earthly joys but toys. He was thirty years old and separated from his wife, whom he suspected of having foisted another man's child on him, perhaps with her father's connivance.[27] The theme of vanity may have resonated

particularly with him because of the early death of his parents, his marital reverses, and the death of friends such as his cousin the Duke of Norfolk.

- Financial troubles and the exorbitant expense of pleasure: Oxford, once possibly the richest man in England, had suffered increasing financial difficulties since his European tour in 1575-76, and by 1580 was in serious financial straits.
- Leisure to write and publish 1577-1580: Oxford had returned from Italy to England by 1577.

His literary interests, experience and acquaintances:

- Oxford had been involved in creating entertainments since his days at Gray's Inn in the 1560s, and during 1577-1580 is known to have created entertainments for Elizabeth's court and to have acted there.
- At a later period (in *Palladis Tamia*, 1598), Francis Meres would praise Oxford for writing plays. We do have one short semi-dramatic piece known to be by Oxford, the "Knight of the Tree of the Sun" tourney speech; however, Meres seems to be talking about longer works.
- Oxford was both a poet and a patron of other writers, including Munday, John Lyly, and Angel Day, all of whom served as his secretaries. In all he is supposed to have been responsible for the publication of about 33 works, and contributed a preface to Bedingfield's edition of *Cardanus His Comfort*.
- Oxford had already published poetry, including poetry in another of Munday's collections. His published poetry, as we will see, shares characteristics with "The Paine of Pleasure."
- Previous publication with non-nobles: Oxford not only had allowed himself to be published previously in his lifetime, but had let his work appear in *The Paradise of Dainty Devices* with a man who had actually worked for him, Thomas Churchyard.[28]
- Acquaintance with Gascoigne: Oxford could well have

been acquainted with Gascoigne through his guardian and father-in-law, Sir William Cecil. (George Gascoigne's wife was related to Cecil's wife's sister.) Gascoigne himself had served Cecil as an agent in France and Flanders in 1576.[29] In addition, there is a Gray's Inn connection: Gascoigne had been at Gray's Inn in 1566, just before Oxford took up his studies there, and Gascoigne's *Supposes* had been produced at Gray's Inn just before Oxford matriculated there.[30] Acquaintance with Gascoigne might have also acquainted him with Nicholas Breton, Gascoigne's stepson.

- Collected works: Oxford did not collect his own works, though it has been suggested that they were collected by his daughter and her husband's family after his death.[31]

His education and studies:

- Divinity: Oxford had studied divinity as part of his education under both Sir Thomas Smith and Sir William Cecil.[32] At the time this poem was published, he had become a secret Catholic and might well have been thinking about divinity. He would renounce Catholicism two months later.
- As Cecil's ward, Oxford had an extensive, well-documented modern education. (The "typical Elizabethan education" sometimes cited to prove what Shakespeare might have learned in Stratford is Cecil's outline for Oxford's education.)
- He had access to Cecil's library, at 1800 volumes one of the largest in England, and to several others; he also had his own library, which had reached 600 volumes by the time he was 16.[33]
- Knowledge of law: Oxford's early tutor, Sir Thomas Smith, was the Regius Professor of Civil Law at Cambridge. Oxford later studied law at Gray's Inn, and throughout his life would be involved in legal questions. Existing letters from him deal with legal issues.
- Knowledge of astronomy: Sir Thomas Smith, Oxford's early tutor, had a strong and lifelong interest in astronomy

and astrology. In 1572 Oxford himself studied with John Dee.

- Music: Oxford was an accomplished performer and a patron of other musicians.[34]
- Dancing: Oxford was known for his dancing; Elizabeth once ordered him to dance to amuse French envoys. (He refused.)
- Bowling: John Stow mentions bowling alleys among the amenities of Fisher's Folly, a house Oxford had bought by February 1580.
- Tennis: Among Oxford's known poems is one comparing love to a game of tennis; Oxford's family seat, Castle Hedingham, was provided with a tennis court,[35] and he famously quarreled with Sir Philip Sidney during a game of tennis.
- Horses: Oxford, three times jousting champion of England, would have been familiar with the training of horses.

Oxford's connection with Munday is worth discussing at length. Oxford had been Munday's patron since the mid-1570s. At Oxford's suggestion, Munday had gone to study the Renaissance in Rome (financing the trip by pretending to be a Catholic convert, and possibly becoming a spy for Cecil in the process).[36] On returning from Rome, Munday became one of Oxford's secretaries and may have been in charge of Oxford's group of players.[37] In 1579, Munday dedicated the *Mutability* poems to Oxford, taking the trouble to compose two anagrams on his name and motto, and apparently based the hero of his *Zelauto* (1580) on Oxford. If Oxford wrote "The Paine of Pleasure", he might well have entrusted it to Munday for publication.[38]

THE POETIC CASE FOR OXFORD

Oxford's characteristics as a poet are similar to those of the poet of "The Paine of Pleasure." As enumerated by Steven May,[39] they include copiousness or amplification, rhetorical questioning, the ABABCC rhyme scheme, alliterative phrasing, and unusual variety of subject. None of these is distinctive but the last—indeed, May can find no tag that unambiguously marks a poem as Oxford's—and copiousness, rhetorical questions, alliteration, and the ABABCC rhyme scheme are common enough in verse of the 1560s and 1570s. However, all of them are to be found in "The Paine of Pleasure."

AMPLIFICATION AND REPETITION

Amplification and repetition are the basic rhetorical strategies of "The Paine of Pleasure" as they are of much of Oxford's work. Repetition includes the "joy/toy" and "delight/despite" rhymes, as well as "What should I need...more to write?" at the conclusion of several chapters. Here is one of many examples of amplification:

> In getting first, the brain is busiéd
> With deep devise to cast a plot to gain:
> Then armes, hands, legs and feet are occupied
> For cankered coin, their strongest joint to strain.
> This is (alas) a wicked way to gain:
> Yet not the worst: for some, oh cursed they
> That seek the mean to have their parents slain...

RHETORICAL QUESTIONS

The poet frequently asks the reader questions to hammer home a rhetorical point:

> And is it not a pretty sport, think you,
> That makes one mad ere he attain the same?

> For beauty first breeds liking in the mind,
> Liking breeds lust, lust lewdness, lewdness, what?

ALLITERATIVE PHRASING

Alliterative phrasing is common in "The Paine of Pleasure":

But wealth so won doth breed no little woe…

As in such sort doth settle our delight:
As doth our wits withdraw from wisdom quite.

FEATURES DISTINCTIVE TO OXFORD'S POETRY

May also finds several characteristics of Oxford's work that are less common in the mid-century, and these also he shares with the poet of "The Paine of Pleasure." These include

- The themes of honor and revenge
- A pervasive secularism and lack of didacticism
- A relatively great range of subject
- Stylistic similarities, including the ABABCC rhyme scheme, iambic pentameter, and run-on lines

HONOR AND REVENGE

Oxford is unusual among Elizabethan poets in writing on the Jacobean themes of honor and revenge. The poet of "The Paine of Pleasure" devotes two of the pleasures, "Honor" and a large section of "Fencing," to them.

Which joy to tell, by name is Honour hie,
Which noblest minds account the greatest joy:
Which first obtained by deadly jeopardy,
They do, God knows, with care enough enjoy.
Oh man most mad to love so vain a thing
As with small joy doth thousand sorrows bring.

SECULARISM AND LACK OF DIDACTICISM

May estimates that didactic poems form a full quarter of all surviving Elizabethan printed verse, but Oxford is not known to have written any,[40] and the poet of "The Paine of Pleasure" shows a similar disinterest in drawing morals. This is especially striking given his subject: Though "The Paine of Pleasure" attempts to be didactic, it constantly slips back toward a psychological secularism. Even the pleasure of the study of divinity are chosen "for joy," for the pleasure of study and as a "soul's salve" rather than for worship or the glory of God.

> Then judge I pray which yields the more delight,
> Divinity, then choose it for thy joy:
> Study that chief, and labour day and night,
> By that to learn to shield thee from annoy.
> And thou shalt find it salveth every sore
> And saves the soul, and what joy can be more?

VARIETY OF SUBJECT MATTER

The subjects of Oxford's verse are more varied than those of other poets; so are those of the poet of "The Paine of Pleasure". If "The Grief of Joy" is actually the inspiration of "The Paine of Pleasure," we may ascribe part of the poem's variety of subject to Gascoigne's example. However, "The Paine of Pleasure" out-Gascoignes Gascoigne, treating more subjects in more detail and with at least equal originality. Wrestling, climbing, tennis, and fishing are uncommon subjects in the poetry of the period—or ever—but the poet of "The Paine of Pleasure" swings easily between the specifics of broken strings and nervous hawks and the painful abstractions of moral values.

STYLISTIC SIMILARITIES

Stylistically, Oxford and the poet of "The Paine of Pleasure" both favor the ABABCC rhyme scheme and iambic pentameter. Oxford's surviving verse uses the ABABCC rhyme scheme and iambic pentameter more than any other form.

His earlier verse shows the same interest in quantitative and irregular stress as does "The Paine of Pleasure". From "Paine":

Ut, re, mi, fa, sol, la and back again

From Oxford:

Framed in the front of forlorn hope...

In this period run-on lines are rare, but both Oxford and the poet of "The Paine of Pleasure" use run-on lines frequently. From "Paine":

And Friends and kinsfolks closely make away
To gain their goods... ("Riches")

By sacred Laws we can confute in kind
The unjust cause... ("Divinity")

Now see how far this study doth surpass
All studies else... ("Divinity")

Some men thereby perhaps do take delight
To make wrong right... ("Law")

From Oxford:

Even as the wax doth melt, or dew consume away
Before the sun...[41]

A crown of bays shall that man wear
That triumphs over me...[42]

And since my mind, my wit, my head, my voice and tongue are weak
To utter, move, devise, conceive, sound forth, declare and speak...[43]

SUMMARY

Oxford's identified poems show strong stylistic similarities to "The Paine of Pleasure." The circumstances of his life match what can be inferred of the author's circumstances. Though "The Paine of Pleasure" is longer and more accomplished than any of Oxford's previously identified poems, nothing in it is startlingly different from Oxford's other work. Oxford is likely to have been acquainted with George Gascoigne, who worked for his father-in-law and whose work may have inspired "The Paine of Pleasure." He certainly knew Anthony Munday, who published it. Finally, alone among identified court poets at this period, Oxford had previously allowed his work to be published in a book with commoner poets, as "The Paine of Pleasure" was.

No other identified poet is as likely to have written the poem as Oxford. His two modern biographers agree that it may reasonably be ascribed to him.

If nothing else, this changes our sense of Oxford as a poet. He was previously known as the author of roughly 20 short poems, as well as a tourney speech, a preface, and plays rumored to have been written by him; he is now also the author of a poem running 1200 lines, 36 pages. At the very least, it makes the existence of the plays more likely.

IS "THE PAINE OF PLEASURE" SHAKESPEAREAN?

Of course, the gold ring of identifying a new Oxford poem— exciting as that is—is not merely identifying a new Oxford poem. Does "The Paine of Pleasure" have anything to say about the Shakespeare authorship controversy?

We must start by asking what we mean by "Shakespearean" in this context. As Michael D. Bristol has perceptively said, Shakespeare's readers have made Shakespeare into a myth.

> Shakespeare's works, together with various ways which people have invented to interact with them, have become durable features in the cultural landscape of contemporary society. The myth of Shakespeare appears as a complex narrative that orients and guides the social activity generated by

these remarkable artifacts. Believing in Shake-
speare is not altogether different from believing in
Santa Claus; such belief articulates a deep sense of
affiliation with a tradition of expressive forms and
institutional practices.[44]

Shakespeare's finished work, published under his name,
stands on a peak not only of its own quality but of its readers'
mythmaking attention. However accomplished "The Paine of
Pleasure" is for its time, however delightfully a handful of its lines
may sing, however historically important it may be, it has received
none of the Shakespearean attention, has not participated in that
"complex narrative...[that] tradition of expressive forms and
institutional practices." And in that sense it cannot be
Shakespearean.

Nor does it speak in the tones of the mature poet. But no
poem of 1580 could. The first datable poem in the Shakespearean
canon was not published until 1593. Between "The Paine of
Pleasure" and *Venus and Adonis* stretch all of Sidney's work,
Spenser's *Shepherd's Calendar* and *The Faerie Queene*, Marlowe's
plays, and the early work of Shakespeare himself. By the time of
Venus and Adonis we are in the Golden Age of the new poetics; in
1580 we are barely at its beginnings.

So we cannot say it is part of the Shakespearean canon—
perhaps because it was not written by the same man who wrote
the known Shakespeare plays and poems; certainly because the
Shakespeare plays and poems are phenomena of the 1590s and
after. To draw a poem of 1580 into that canon would weight it with
expectations it cannot fulfill.

We can only consider what elements of "The Paine of
Pleasure" might have similarities with later work published as by
Shakespeare.

GENERAL STYLISTIC SIMILARITIES

We have already mentioned the ABABCC rhyme scheme,
which Shakespeare shares with many other poets including
Oxford. The rhythm of the poem is iambic pentameter, not as

common as it would be later in the century, but not uncommon.

Rhetorical questioning, repetition, run-on lines, and alliterative phrasing are all Shakespearean as well.

Shakespeare uses run-on lines more frequently than most writers of this period; however, his known work dates from later than this poem, when run-on lines were more common.

The use of repetition is somewhat more distinctive. Shakespeare frequently repeats a word several times within a few lines, using both sense and rhythm to vary the repetition. The poet of "The Paine of Pleasure" uses the same trick:

> 'Tis not the thing, but the delight therein
> That makes or mars, delights or grieveth sore.
> Then take good heed when first you do begin
> To take delight in any kind of thing,
> For too much joy doth after sorrow bring.
> ("Tennis")

The size of the poem is also distinctive. Though one may argue that the poem is essentially a collection of shorter poems, the sheer bulk and coherence of it is characteristic of a writer who is comfortable with longer works.

CLASS ATTITUDES

Walt Whitman notoriously remarked that Shakespeare's sympathies were with "the wolfish earls." Critics have disagreed, but Shakespeare's work undeniably draws its principal characters largely from the upper classes. The peasantry and the serving classes are treated with Shakespeare's generous humanity, but they are seldom major characters.

The poet of "The Paine of Pleasure" also sees country "louts" from the outside. But more distinctively, he has a similar brusque sympathy with them, and he does not make them into generic pastoral figures. His ship's boy is just a boy doing a dangerous job, and falls into the sea with no "pleasant conceits" or comparisons with Icarus:

Even so in ship, the boy that seeks to climb,
By cords and lines, if either rope do slip
Or hand or foot, as many do sometime,
Then down amain he falls into the ship
Or in the Sea, where hundred then to one
He never scapes, there's one young Seaman gone.
("Climbing")

MORAL ATTITUDES

For both the poet of "The Paine of Pleasure" and Shakespeare, pleasure, beauty, and love are snares not only in the moral but in the psychological realm. Both speak of spending money freely and suffering the consequences. Both live uneasily between the secular and the spiritual. Neither is entirely convinced of the efficacy of prayer. Neither is didactic or moralizing, in an age when didactic and moralizing poetry was common and valued.

Both connect good humor and a good heart, a sullen mood and an evil nature. The distinction for both is almost one of grace or essential nature vs. intellect, "kind" against mind. Shakespeare prefers Falstaff's disreputable grace to Malvolio's moralizing self-delusion; the poet of "The Paine of Pleasure" distinguishes the essential nature of a man from his fallible understanding.

...For wantonness and wickedness are two:
'Tis not the grace in any, but the mind
That moves a man, or good or bad to do...
("Music")

It is a subtle attitude, and not a common one.

CHOICE OF CONTENT

The content of "The Paine of Pleasure" is consistent with its being Shakespeare's.

Shakespeare writes often and movingly on honor and revenge. One could never compare Shakespeare's great honor-ridden characters in *Othello* and *Hamlet* with the discussions of honor in "The Paine of Pleasure," but there is the same sense that honor is a necessity.

Shakespeare uses proper terms properly from the law and medicine, as does the author of "The Paine of Pleasure."

Shakespeare's astronomy is educated and exact; the author of "The Paine of Pleasure" takes pleasure in studying astronomy.

Music is a common reference in Elizabethan poetry and plays, but Shakespeare shares with the author of "The Paine of Pleasure" more specific preferences. Neither likes "fiddlers":[45]

> And there I stood amazed for a while,
> As on a pillory, looking through the lute,
> While she did call me rascal fiddler
> And twangling Jack, with twenty such vile terms,
> As she had studied to misuse me so.
> (*Taming of the Shrew*, II, i)

But both men care deeply for good music; the poet of "The Paine of Pleasure" "cannot well reprove" court music even to prove his point.

Shakespeare's works contain many references to hawking and metaphors relating to hawking; the poet of "The Paine of Pleasure" not only uses the Elizabethan commonplace hawking terms (eyas, haggard) but makes educated distinctions among long- and short-winged hawks, falcons, tercels, lanners, lannerets, sparhawks, and merlins.[46]

Both poets know the sports of the nobility. Shakespeare sets scenes on tennis courts and has casual tennis references; "The Paine of Pleasure" contains a section on tennis. Elizabethan tennis courts were privately owned and it was a rich man's game; "of all sports, tennis is a costly game," the poet of "The Paine of Pleasure" says. Bowling was a relatively new sport in England (the first *OED* reference dates from the time of King Henry VIII), and, as Shakespeare indicates, it was also an expensive sport played principally by rich men and nobles. But Shakespeare knows the terminology and rules as intricately as does the author of "The Paine of Pleasure."

CLOTEN Was there ever man had such luck! When I kiss'd the jack, upon an up-cast to be hit away! I had a hundred pound on't; and the n a whoreson jackanapes must take me up for swearing, as if I borrowed mine oaths of him, and might not spend them at my pleasure.

(*Cymbeline*, II, i)

RARE AND NEW WORDS

Shakespeare is known for the size of his vocabulary and the number of words he introduced into English or first used in their modern sense. In part this is a phenomenon of Shakespeare's eminence—the compilers of the *OED* paid more attention to Shakespeare than to, say, Thomas Churchyard—and the popularity of the plays has popularized some of his words.

But the phenomenon is real: Shakespeare made up words, or found uncommon ones around him, and used them in his poetry. So does the poet of "The Paine of Pleasure."

Both poets are particularly fond of words relating to sports; indeed, the poet of "The Paine of Pleasure" finds words one of the few pleasures that cause no pain. The author revels not only in fencing and archery, but in the "terms" one can use around them.

What sport it is to see an arrow fly,
A gallant archer cleanly draw his bow,
In shooting off, again how cunningly
He hath his loose, in letting of it go:
To nock it sure, and draw it to the head
And then fly out, hold straight, and strike it dead
With other terms that archers long have used,
As blow wind, stoupe,[47] ah, down the wind a bow...
("Shooting")

By Fencing grows our terms of the Bravado[48],
Our foins and thrusts, the deadly stab and all:
Which some more finely[49] call a Stabbado[50],
And some a blow, a cleanly wipe can call.

And some a rake, that crosseth both the shins,
Now with such stuff this joyful sport begins...
With other terms that were too long to tell...
("Fencing")

In some of the sports poems, notably "Fishing" and "Fowling", the author confesses himself to be unsympathetic to the sport itself: but, oh, the words! The author of "The Paine of Pleasure" uses every one of his terms accurately, and he takes a collector's pleasure in listing them. From "Fishing" come *trammel, drag, bow line, shotterel*[51], *weel*[52], and the early use of *gentill* to mean a maggot or bluebottle larva used as bait.[53] "Fowling" produces *snipe*[54], the distinction between *snipe* and *snite*[55], and "shooluerd" (probably *shovelard*, a spoonbill). "Bowling" brings in *bias, rub* and *crank*, as well as an extended metaphor taken from bowling:

How some delight to see a round Bowl run
Smoothly away, until he catch a rub:[56]
Then hold thy bias[57], if that cast were won,
The game were up as sure then as a club.[58]
Then upright Bowls, that neede not any bank,
And for a game, a fine throw in the crank.

But if they marked[59] their money run away,
Their coin to cross quite bias from their purse,
'Twould make them leave that costly kind of play[60]...

"Music" takes in a rich haul of terminology:

By Larges and Longs, by Breefes and Semibreefes.[61]
Minims, Crochets, Quavers, Sharps, Flats, to fain...

Brick-wall, from "Tennis", is an especially interesting term since it provides another possible biographical hint. The *OED* quotes Cotgrave's definition, 1611: a brick-wall is "a side-stroake at Tennis wherein the ball goes not right forward, but hits one of the walls of the court, and thence bounds towards the avuerse partie." It is also used figuratively. The term existed in French and Italian before it came (briefly) into English; the *OED* cites Florio, 1598, who still uses the Italian term *briccola*.[62] The first cited use of the English term, *brickwall*, dates from the same year as "The Paine of Pleasure," 1580, in Claudius Hollyband's *Treasury of the French Tongue*.[63] We can thus deduce the poet of "The Paine of Pleasure" might have played tennis in France or Italy, where the term was more common, and/or might have known Hollyband. Hollyband had appeared in *The Paradise of Dainty Devices* with Oxford in1576, and Oxford had spent time in both France and Italy, where he almost certainly played tennis.[64]

One can go on: *capri*[65] and *cross point*[66] from "Dancing", *swasher*[67] from "Fencing"; but it is unnecessary to pile example on example. The poet of "The Paine of Pleasure", like Shakespeare, has a large vocabulary of new and modern words and of specialized terms, and he likes to use metaphors from sports.

DRAMATIC VOICES, RHYTHMIC EXPERIMENTATION

Lyric poetry is thick on the ground in the Elizabethan age, but in the poetry of 1580, true dramatic voices are rare. Gascoigne can make his own voice into poetry; later, Marlowe and Webster will reach heights of pure dramatic voice. "I'll burn my books—ah, Mephistophilis!" "Cover her face. Mine eyes dazzle. She died young." But the effect of transcribing the ordinary voices of human beings, in prose or verse, comes into English drama overwhelmingly from Shakespeare. "Put up your bright swords, or the dew will rust them," Othello says to the young soldiers. It is a spare intense poetry that rises from the way men talk, from sabotaging the regular ratchet of iambic pentameter in the interest of characterization.

The poet of "The Paine of Pleasure" can just barely be mentioned in Shakespeare's company. Occasionally, very occasionally, we can hear voices, and for a moment a character rises out of the lines. We hear an Elizabethan fencing master instructing a pupil:

> Lie here, lie there, strike out your blow at length,
> Strike and thrust with him, look to your dagger

hand:
Believe me sir, you bear a gallant strength,
But choose your ground, at vantage where to
stand...

or a group of women gossiping about bad luck as they fly their hawks:

It is my luck, what most delighteth me
Comes to some mischief one or other way...

This facility for voices is supported by what we have previously seen of the poet's taste for run-on lines, quantitative meter, and rhythmic experimentation. None of these are common in the verse of the 1570s, though they are characteristic of Shakespeare from the very beginning of what we can recognize as Shakespeare.

SUMMARY

Of course we cannot say that "The Paine of Pleasure" is by the same man who wrote the Shakespeare canon. Too many years and too many literary questions separate this poem from any known Shakespearean work. And it is journeyman poetry, like the wavery engravings that William Blake published in magazines during the 1780s, with only an occasional certainty of line to suggest the world-changing work of decades later.

But if we were looking for Shakespeare's early work, this kind of journeyman poetry is exactly what we might find.

We can say that there is nothing internal to the poem that would prevent this from being an early work by the same man who wrote the Shakespeare plays. We can even say, more strongly, that certain characteristics of Shakespeare's work—not the most obvious, nor the easiest to imitate—are shared by the poet of "The Paine of Pleasure."

And in that sense the poem is Shakespearean.

Theoretically, "The Paine of Pleasure," if it were written in 1580, could even be by William Shakespeare of Stratford. It is hugely unlikely that a sixteen-year-old poet, who in 1580 was living in Stratford or Lancashire as an apprentice or servant, could have produced twelve hundred lines that could be taken for court verse. But genius is unlikely. Shakespeare could do things no other poet dreamed of; he could theoretically have done this.

However, it is almost impossible that Anthony Munday would have published it. On the basis of any known facts about Shakespeare's or Munday's lives, one cannot explain how an early poem by an unknown young man, who had never been in London, could have become the title poem of a collection edited by an experienced London-based anthologist. Munday was editing for profit; he knew London writers; he was not that desperate.

But, if "The Paine of Pleasure" is Oxford's—and that case is strong—its appearance in an anthology edited by his secretary is not surprising. Moreover, it may indicate Oxford's goals as a poet. His appearance in two anthologies addressed to the common reader suggests that he might have had an interest in addressing this audience, an interest that might have also led him to write or adapt plays for the common theater.

Reattributing "The Paine of Pleasure" is significant. We can no longer consider Oxford the author only of a handful of early poems. As the author of "The Paine of Pleasure", Oxford is a substantial poet, whose extant verse is not incompatible with the claim that he may have written Shakespeare.

...WHERE TO GO NEXT?

So we come back to my hero, Joe Roper, who looked for journeyman Shakespearean poetry in *Sir Thomas More* and found it—perhaps—in "The Paine of Pleasure". If you got this far, you may go on and read the poem, and you may well decide Joe was wrong.

But if you read the poem and are still intrigued—

If you are, there is a logical and interesting consequence. I hardly dare mention it, because it goes against all the accepted wisdom of Shakespeare studies.

The accepted wisdom says that it is impossible to find new, undiscovered work by Shakespeare. There are no Shakespeare manuscripts, except perhaps that scribbled page and a half of *More*. All the Shakespeare apocrypha are forgeries or wishful thinking.

One cannot find more information about Shakespeare's working life as a writer, his literary friendships, the influences that shaped him. We would all like to do it, but it's just not possible.

I will now immolate my claims to wisdom. Perhaps it is possible.

The current state of Shakespeare studies is constrained. The constraint is that any significant material must be found in England, because Shakespeare seems to have travelled nowhere else, and any early work by Shakespeare must date from about 1588 or later. Any influences or friendships must be appropriate to a professional actor and friend of Richard Field, rather than, for instance, to a courtier and friend of Elizabeth.

What if one were to spread the net wider?

Then one would have almost the whole Elizabethan period to look at. The earliest proposed datable reference in Shakespeare comes as early as 1562. (Hamlet tells Polonius "You are a fishmonger," possibly referring to Cecil's Wednesday fast bill of 1562.) Casting the net that far back allows one to look, for instance, at the influence of the world-changing nova of 1573 on the metaphorical structure of *Hamlet*, from the baleful star in the first scene to the location of the play and the names of Rosencrantz and Guildenstern. What else might one find in the 1570s and early 1580s?

Shakespeare, notoriously, left no record of his literary acquaintances, but casting the net wider suggests some possible research areas:

- Munday seems to deserve a longer look than I have given him. For instance, there is a strange and interesting sketch of Shakespeare's history plays in Munday's *Watch-Woord to England* (1584).

- Nicholas Breton has several poems in his *Works of a Young Wit* (1577), describing poetic games at an unnamed noble's house; this sounds temptingly like what supposedly happened a few years later at Fisher's Folly. Mining Breton's other works might turn up something.
- Angel Day includes an amusing sketch of a Falstaffian servant in *The English Secretorie* (1586), and there are several other remarkably good letters; The English Secretorie may reward study.
- John Lyly's relationship with Shakespeare deserves a second look—it seems odd that Shakespeare parodied Lyly so long after he was popular.
- George Gascoigne, Thomas Churchyard, and even Thomas Bedingfield may reward study.

Spreading the net beyond England would open up the ample material available on Shakespeare's knowledge of Italy, and suggest more new places to search: for instance, the Medici archives and the Venetian libraries. There has been some very interesting work done by Italian Shakespeare scholars on Shakespeare's knowledge of Italy; it deserves to be taken seriously in spite of the fact that it says he almost certainly was there. Similar work should be done on France.

And if Shakespeare were involved with the world of the courtiers, one might find interesting material in the royal collections or in the remaining great private libraries, particularly the library of the Cecil family.

Why not?

Suppose there were to be a scholar trained in professional methodology and standards of proof. Suppose that person were to know at least small Latin and less Greek, could read secretary hand, and had a working knowledge of Renaissance Italian and French. Suppose they had a good grounding in stylometrics, in the clear-headed way that Brian Vickers or Patrick Juola has demonstrated that stylometrics can be used. Suppose that person were to have all the background required for a standard career in Shakespeare studies. But suppose that person, daringly, were to cast his or her net wider, looking for Shakespeare in the private archives, or in the early 1580s or even late 1570s, or in Italy, in all the places where we have been told Shakespeare cannot possibly be.

What could they find?

The pleasure of finding a new Shakespeare poem, like all other pleasures, is not necessarily lasting; as "The Paine of Pleasure" warns, "take good heed when first you do begin/To take delight in any kind of thing." But it is indeed a pleasure. Don Foster attests to it, and Gary Taylor, and I do too. To find something in the archives, to hear through four hundred years of obscurity a poetic voice—even if one is eventually proved wrong—is an experience worth having. And it adds something, no matter how small, to what is known about Shakespeare and his time.

And if that poetic voice were indeed to be Shakespeare's—

If one is to be Quixotic about anything, one can't do better than chasing Shakespeare.

If you are that scholar, I wish you success in the hunt. May you have joy.

May you find Shakespeare.

O fond delight, oh grieuous kinde of ioy,
Oh cankred coyne, the cause of deadly paine:
Oh madhead man to ioy in such a toy,
Oh greedie mindes that so doe grope for gaine.
  Oh wretched wealth, whose ioy dooth breede such wo,
  Oh God forgiue such fooles as seeke it so.

THE   PAINE   OF   PLEASURE:
MODERNIZED ANNOTATED TEXT

When I sometimes begin to weigh in mind
The wretched state of miserable man,
Me thinks (alas) I presently do find
Such sudden harms that happen now and then
As every way do plainly seem to show
That man doth live within a world of woe.

For first in birth we work our mother's woe,
In infancy we cause our Parents care:
In further years we wander to and fro
From virtue's line, and light in sinful snare.
[In further years XX68], we fall in misery,
And last in age, God knoweth how we die.[69]

In childish years, we first with cries begin
To shew in age such sorrows as ensue:
In lusty youth, we daily travail in

Such wicked ways as wicked age doth rue.
In such a sort our elder years we spend
As in our age doth[70] breed our doleful end.

And for the joys that in our life we find,
Which are but few, and yet not free from woe:
What are they all, but Feathers in the wind
Which every tempest tosseth to and fro?
Which tempests so are rising every day
As in short space blow all our joys away.

And now such joys as we short time enjoy
From tender years, even till our dying hour:
Which many ways are mixed with annoy
So that each sweet doth yield as sharp a sour,
Mark what they be, as I do shew them plain,
And you may see, each pleasure's fruit is pain.

In infancy, what is our chiefest joy?
The Nurse's dug, whose milk may mar the Child:
And then delight in many a gaudy toy,
Whose garish hue doth make our wits so wild
As in such sort doth settle our delight:
As doth our wits withdraw from wisdom quite,

Then to be dandled in our mother's lap,
And to be stroked at cock'ring[71] Father's hand:
When better were by now and then a rap
For to be kept in true obedience' band,
Then to be cocked of both our Parents so
As that in years it turn unto our woe.

For Mothers mild, that think they love the child
By keeping him from Fathers' cruelty,
In time of years may find themselves[72] beguiled
By letting him have lavish liberty.
For liberty in youth doth run such race
As quite forgets the path of perfect grace.

And then (alas) too late comes 'Had I wist,'
And then they blame the nature of the Child:
Which they might well have bridled as they list,
But wantonness hath made the wits so wild
As rather runs in vale of vanity
Than seeks the path of perfect piety.

But let me leave to speak of childish years,
And let me write of lusty gallant youth,
Who through the world doth travail with his peers
Such ways in age as moves his mind to ruth.
And in such toys doth set his chief delight
As that in age doth work his utter spite.

BEAUTY, THE FIRST PLEASURE.

For now behold in youth one chiefest joy,
In which too many most delight do find:
Which though well weighed is but indeed a toy,
Yet to delight allures the wisest mind.
Which thing to name is Beauty's heavenly hue:
Which yields delight that thousands daily rue.

For beauty first breeds liking in the mind,
Liking breeds lust, lust lewdness, lewdness, what?
Such world of woes as age doth quickly find,
And cries (alas) repentance all too late.
See beauty then, in youth the chiefest joy,
In age is seen to work no small annoy.

Beauty in some doth cause a kind of pride,
And pride must be maintainéd all by cost:
And cost makes youth in age his head to hide
For shame or debt, when all his wealth is lost.
But oh fond youth to joy in Beauty so

As that in age his joy doth breed such woe.

In other some yet Beauty worketh worse,
It makes access of such as practice ill:
Whose ill access the beautiful may curse,
That unto vice allure their wanton will.
Oh vile delight, where Beauty so is placed,
To make indeed the fairest face disgraced.

In some again it breeds a great delight,
In modest[73] minds, whose hearts are not at rest,
But thousand pangs are daily forced to prove
For loving them whom beauty so hath blest.
For luckless lots so follow lovers' joy
As many ways doth work them great annoy.

But where the face with beauty is bedecked,
And bears withal a modest countenance,
Whose mind again to virtue hath respect,
And thereby seeks their state for to advance,
There will I say it is no foolish toy:
But thought indeed a rare and heavenly joy.

But to be short, in youth our chief delight,
As first I said, in Beauty's heavenly hue,
As well in youth as age works[74] such despite
As well may make the stoutest heart to rue,
Which now I leave, and to some other toy
Which yields great woe, but to a little joy.

RICHES, THE SECOND PLEASURE.

In Riches now, another kind of joy,[75]
In which both youth and age have great delight:
Were it well weighed, and it were but a toy,
Which many ways do breed their great despite.

In getting first with labour, care and pain,
In keeping too[76] as great unrest again.

In getting first, the brain is busiéd
With deep devise to cast a plot to gain:
Then arms, hands, legs and feet are occupied
For cankered[77] coin, their strongest joint to strain.
I do not mean, as some unwisely do,
Devise[78] for coin, to strain a neck joint too:

God forbid that, and yet some men do so,
Both stretch and crack, and break their neck joint too:
But wealth so won doth breed no little woe,
God mend their minds that so devise to do.
Better to die a beggar of the twain:
Then by such means to seek or gape for gain.

This is (alas) a wicked way to gain:
Yet not the worst: for some, oh cursed they,
That seek the mean to have their parents slain
And Friends and kinsfolks closely make away
To gain their goods, but oh, ill gotten gain
Whose getting breeds the soul eternal pain.

God shield each one from such a beastly thought
So to devise, to purchase worldly prey
And pardon those that wickedly have wrought
Such dev'lish means to work their souls' decay
And grant us all so for to seek for wealth
As necks crack not, nor hinder our souls' health.

But leaving these, let's see some other ways
In making means to hoard up heaps of pence:
In strange devise to spend both night and days,
And leave their home, and go a great way hence.
To find such stuff, as to return again,
Do yield them small amends for all their pain.

Some sail by sea to seek out foreign soil,
To find out there some gem of value[79] great.
In seeking which, with tough and tedious toil
To save themselves, they oft are fain to sweat
And ere their Barks be safe arrived on land
How oft their lives in thousand dangers stand.

And let their ships be safely set on shore,
And they do find that which they look for there,
Yet ere return they live perplexed sore,
With troubled mind, now sailing half in fear
Of foreign foes. of tempests, Rocks, or Sands,
Or falling into roving Pirates' hands.

And let them be returned home with joy,
And all their goods brought home to their desire:
Yet see what then doth work their hearts annoy,
Oh then they fear each foolish spark of fire
Should burn their house, and then another grief,
Each Mouse that peeps should surely be a thief.

Some other now that love to live at home,
And only seek by sweat of brow to gain:
With spade and shovel[80] about the fields they roam,
Turmoiling still with labour sore and pain
With cark and care to purchase wealth in haste:
Which God he knows but little time will last.

Some seek by play at Tables, Cards, and Dice,
In secret sort a world of wealth to win:
But who seek so do prove themselves unwise
In losing all before their gain begin.
Whose hope of gain can never breed such joy
As certain loss doth breed their hearts' annoy.

What should I write of every strange devise
That some men use in seeking worldly pelf?
The proverb says that no man can be wise

That is not wise each way to help himself.
But scripture says the rich to Heaven on high
Go[81] like a Camel through a Needle's eye.

And let a man grow rich in lusty youth,
And have for wealth almost the world at will,
Yet see in age, God wot too great a ruth,
It breedeth death full sore against their will.
How joys he then? in being his own friend:
To bring his life, his chiefest joy, to end.

O fond delight, oh grievous kind of joy,
Oh cankered coin, the cause of deadly pain:
Oh madhead[82] man to joy in such a toy,
Oh greedy minds that so do grope for gain.
Oh wretched wealth, whose joy doth breed such woe,
Oh God forgive such fools as seek it so.

But let wealth pass, one other joy I find,
Which many count their great and chiefest joy,
Which if they would once wisely weigh in mind,
They soon should see it plainly but a toy.
Which when God wot with great ado[83] they gain,
Yet being got, it is not free from pain.

HONOUR, THE THIRD PLEASURE.

Which joy to tell by name is Honour hie,[84]
Which noblest minds account the greatest joy:
Which first obtained, by deadly jeopardy
They do, God knows, with care enough enjoy.
Oh man most mad to love so vain a thing
As with small joy doth thousand sorrows bring.

Lo, first the care in seeking how to climb,
With study strange how it doth beat our brain:

In climbing then our observance of time,
Then heed to hold, least we go down again.
The fear to fall,[85] and if we fall, what then?
But fear of death, which haps to many men.

Let us scape death, yet may we break a bone,
Or lame a limb, or bruise us inwardly,
Or catch a clap may make our hearts to groan
And breed our death, although not presently.
Let us miss these, and have no harm at all:
Yet will it be a grief to take a fall.

And if again, they venture for to climb,
Then must they be more wary than before:
For if they chance to fall the second time,
Tis ten to one but they are bruised sore.
Yet if they live and seek to climb again,
And third time fall, that brings a deadly pain.

Now sundry men devise a sundry mean
To make their way to Honour to attain:
What two will choose, the third misliketh clean,
And glory seeks another way to gain.
But he that seeks the best way that he can:
Shall find unsought some sorrow now and then.

And now and then such sorrows as indeed,
If every man would wisely weigh in mind,
We soon should see how far they do exceed
The little joys that we by honour find.
Oh mind most vain, to seek so vain a joy:
Which many ways doth work so great annoy.

And now, as men do sundry means devise
To scale the top of Honour's stately throne:
So do their sorrows diverse ways arise,
Which makes their minds to make a sundry moan.
Some sigh and sob in secret sort alone:

To make their grief unto the world unknown.

For lo, some men do seek, by force of arms,
To gain the honor of a valiant Knight:
Which by ill hap unto their daily harms
Do find a foe to vanquish them in fight.
In seeking then to climb to Honour so,
Or death or maim doth breed their deadly woe.

Some other seek by Riches to attain,
Even in the top of Honour high to sit:
But climbing up, Fates sling them down again,
As men indeed for such a place unfit.
Which if they fall, and riches fall withal:
Weigh then what grief doth fret them at the gall.

Some fondly think by wasting wealth to gain
The honour due to liberality:
Which contrary unto their pinching pain
Get the dispraise of prodigality.
Which when (alas) their wealth is gone and spent,
Oh think how then their follies they lament.

But let these men that seek for honour so,
As first the Knight that seeks by force of arms
T'obtain the same, yet see his after woe,
In midst of joy, unto his deadly harms
Another comes that is of greater might:
And dispossesses him of honour quite.[86]

Oh then by loss the grief doth far exceed
His little joy in keeping of the same:
Even so the Churl that by his pence indeed
May win a while the Fort of noble fame.
Yet unawares such fortune may befall
That he may lose both Honour, coin and all.

And then what grief the covetous conceive

By loss of coin, their great and chiefest joy:
A man that hath but one eye may perceive
That nothing more can breed their hearts' annoy.
And though their grief of honour lost be least,
Yet who would part with honour once possessed?

Now they that do by spending free obtain
Of many men perhaps a noble name:
Yet noble minds can find no greater pain
Then want of wealth for to maintain the same.
Whose falling so doth work them much despite
As doth their hearts bereave of all delight.

But who would seek the perfect way to climb
To Honour's throne, and surely there to sit:
Must wisely seek with observance of time
By Virtue's line the ready way to hit.
For Virtue gains in life a noble name:
And after death immortal noble Fame.

Virtue is it that only yieldeth joy,
A joy besides that ever will endure:
And such a joy as worketh no annoy,
But doth indeed a heavenly joy procure.
Oh joy of joys, by thee God grant us all
To climb to Heaven, and never thence to fall.

But let me leave of Honour now to write,
And speak my mind of meaner kind of joys:
Which to some minds do give a great delight,
Yet wisely weighed, are nothing else but toys.
And with their joys, which are but small indeed,
What woes they work, which far their joys exceed.

LOVE, THE FOURTH PLEASURE.

Of little joys, behold this first for one,

Some Ladies' love do count a heavenly joy:
In seeking which, some are so woebegone,
As hearts consume with grief and great annoy.
And some have been in love so over shoes,[87]
As lack or loss makes them their lives to lose.

For sundry men by sundry means do seek
Their Lady's love or liking to procure,
And what they think, that may their fancies keep,
That must they do, what pain they so endure.
What gem so rare may please their mistress' eye:
Cost lands and life, but Lovers daily buy.

And let wealth waste, then love begins to shrink,
And when love shrink, then farewell lover's joy:
Then wretched wights in sorrow so must sink,
And worthy well to joy in such a toy.
As so to seek and labour day by day
To purchase that doth breed their own decay.

See then by love, what cost, what care, what woe?
In getting first, and keeping then with pain:
In getting first, what daily griefs do grow,
In losing then, what more despite again.
Oh madhead man, to joy in such a thing:
And with small joy, doth thousand sorrows bring.

HORSES, HAWKS, AND DOGS, THE FIFTH PLEASURE

And so I leave to write of Lovers' joy,
Which many ways doth work a world of woe:
And I will now speak of some other joy,
Which with small joy, doth diverse sorrows sow.
As Horses, Hawks, hounds, birds of diverse sorts,
Which to some minds do make delightful sports.

As first, behold the stately stamping Steed,
That snuffs and snorts, and stamps upon the ground,[88]
I must confess a joyful sight indeed,
But he that hath the toil and labour found
In bringing him unto that pass at first
Will think of joys, the joy in horse the worst.

Now he again that never takes the pain
To break him so, but have him broke to hand,
I think indeed hath more joy of the twain,
In stately sort to see him stamping stand.
But if he take delight to ride him too,
Let him take heed what then he seeks to do.

For such a joy may hap to breed such woe,
By jollity in riding without skill,
That he by fall may catch so sore a blow
As down on ground may make him lie there still,
Where broken bones, limb lamed, or bruises sore
Will make him joy in prancing horse no more.

And if again he chance to sit him fast,
Whereby he may the more increase his joy:
Yet is he not assured his joy will last,
But it will turn unto his great annoy.
For by ill hap his horse may fall sore sick,
Or halt down right, by shoeing ill, or prick.[89]

Perchance again he ride him till he sweat,
And set him up unwalked, somewhat hot:
And so do make him catch so sore a heat
As ten to one if shortly he die not.
And if he die, then farewell Master's joy:
And Rider's pains, and farewell foolish toy.

HAWKS.

So joy in Hawks, good Lord how some delight

To see them kill a bird of meaner strength:
Some mark the pitch[90] in making of their flight,
Some love the Hawk that flieth out at length.
Some most of all the short winged Hawk esteem,
Some long winged Hawks the bravest birds do deem.

Some love to see the Goshawk[91] roughly rush
Thorow the woods, and perch from tree to tree,
And seize upon the Pheasant in the bush,
And sure it is a pretty sport to see.
But in respect of any worthy joy:
God knows it is but even a very toy.

But let it be to some a great delight,
Yet see what toil it daily brings withal:
First, if she take a gadding[92] in her flight,
Then ride and run, and mar Horse, man and all.
And tire themselves to seek a foolish Kite,
Yet lose her too, and then what greater spite?

And let her be the finest Hawk that is,
And never gad, nor have ill qualities,
And what she flies at, seeld[93] or never miss,
Yet is she not quite free from jeopardies.
Some foolish thorn may strike a-two her wing,
And flying marred, then farewell foolish thing.

What should I need of other Hawks to write?
As Falcon, Tassel[94], Lanner, and Lanneret[95],
With little Hawks that Ladies take delight,
Fine Falconer-like upon their fist to set,
As Sparhawk, Merlin, birds I must confess
For Ladies fit, I can well say no less.

But of all Hawks, those Hawks are yet the worst,
For if they catch a bruise abroad in flight,
Then tender hearts, straight into tears they burst
For losing of a little peevish Kite.

A goodly thing to give such cause of joy
As being lost, should breed so great annoy.

Now some again it is a sport to see
What moan they make, some first will sighing say:
'It is my luck, what most delighteth me
Comes to some mischief one or other way.'
And some will say, 'My froward dream tonight
Pretended me this day some foul despite.'

But let me leave of Beasts and birds to write,
And let me now unto some other joys:
Which with delight do breed as great despite,
Which wisely weighed, may well be thought but toys.
As dancing, singing, wrestling, leaping too:
Which who almost but doth delight to do.

Which pleasant sports, ere they be well attained,
Do breed some pain to them that seek the same:
And some of them ere they be thoroughly[96] gained,
Do often strike some limb or other lame.
I will not say, though some have found it so:
Some of their sports do breed their deadly woe.

MUSIC, THE SIXTH PLEASURE.

But let me first of Music speak my mind,
Which with some sport doth yield as great a spite,
The little Boy first by his ears doth find
In plainsong pulls is very small delight.
In prick-song then, a privy pinch or two
Makes him in song have little mind unto.[97]

And weigh the time that wantonly ye spend
First in the Notes, and then again in Clefs:
How to ascend, and then again descend,
By Larges and Longs, by Breefes and Semibreefes.[98]

Minims, Crochets, Quavers, Sharps, Flats, to fain:[99]
Ut, re, me, fa, sol, la, and back again.

Then when you know your notes and how to sing,
Then instruments of Music must be had:
And then an ear to every sundry string,
Which makes some men, myself have seen half mad.
For earnest hearkening to the Music's sound
Makes some oft times too far in Music drowned.

And is it not a pretty sport, think you,
That makes one mad ere he attain the same?
I take it so, and this believe me now,
Who seeks himself to Music's art to frame,
And very young is set to Music's school,
In other arts proves commonly a fool.

It is a sport of troth sometime to see
A right Musician in his formal grace:
How he can look as if it were not he
Especially, when that he is in place.
Whereas he thinks himself to be the best:
For pride or praise, how he can strain his breast.

But if there come another into place
Better then he, then down his feathers fall:
Then Francis Fiddler, with his formal face,
Shrinketh aside and gets him next the wall.
And for a pound he sings not one Note more
Where comes a better than he was before:

But what? me thinks that some begins to frown
To write so much in Fiddler's foul dispraise:
Why, if there be some such odd fiddling Clown,
As plays at Hertford on the Holidays[100]
And takes the matter so much in disgrace:
For all his Fiddle, fart in his fool's face.

For such Musicians make[101] some Minions meet
With their sweet hearts on some ungracious[102] green:
Where after each hath other friendly greet,
Somewhat haps else that may not there be seen.
As bargains made that must be greed upon
Behind some bush, when all the crew[103] is gone.

But let me leave off loutish Music now
To write more words, and let me somewhat say
Of Courtly Music, which I say to you
I cannot well reprove in any way.
Although perhaps some wantons thereby find
A time to play the wantons in their kind.

I mean no harm in that I say in kind,
For wantonness and wickedness are two:
'Tis not the grace in any, but the mind
That moves a man or good or bad to do.
A merry mind a gentle nature shows
When sullen looks are signs of surly shrows.[104]

And yet do some perhaps in dancing deem
That Lovers then have time of great delight,
But if two love one Lady, it must seem
The one's delight, the other's great despite.
And if but one, yet then his present joy
May turn in time unto as great annoy.

For then perhaps he reaps good countenance,
Good words, and more, perhaps with all good will:
Besides, he hath good licence in his dance,
Without suspect to look and talk his fill
And to receive great favour of his friend,
Which when his Dance is done, are all at end.

And then (alas) consider what despite
He bides to think upon his pleasures past:
And sees again his sweet and whole delight

With posting speed to fade away so fast,
No greater grief I think can fortune frame
Than win delight, and then to lose the same.

DANCING, THE SEVENTH PLEASURE.

And touching now the harms that often hap
To such as seek for to be excellent:
In Dancing catch some time so sore a clap[105]
By froward falls, as makes them to repent
The tumbling tricks, and turning on the toe,
When legs do grow so lame they cannot go.

And some brave youths will labour day and night
Till they have got the Caprey[106] and cross point[107]:
But tell me now, how much will they delight
When that they see their legs crossed out of joint?
Or else perhaps with some untoward fall:
Then break their arm, or sometime neck and all.

Oh then behold in Dancing what delight,
Which breeds the Dancer's oft untimely end:
And for myself, I see such great despite
By dancing grow, as he that were my friend,
Sure I would wish him leave all dancing quite
Then in such toys to take so great delight.

Besides, sometime in dancing we do see
Quarrels arise, yea, betwixt friend and friend:
Which once begun, God knows but seldom be
Without great hurt brought unto quiet end.
Consider then the great and dire despite
In dancing grows, in midst of most delight.

What should I need of dancing more to write?
First of the pains in learning how to dance:
And then again how great and foul despite

In dancing oft to many men doth chance.
Let this suffice, it is but e'en a toy,
Whose use may yield a pleasure or annoy.

For least I should seem to dispraise it quite,
In praise of dancing thus much will I say,
Who knows indeed how for to use it right.
May dance full well, I will not say him nay.
For so it is an honest exercise:
And one indeed of courtly qualities.

But for to set in dancing such delight,
As it should seem, to give great cause of joy:
Who deems it so, they are deceived quite,
For God he knows, it is but even a toy.
And such a toy as sure esteemed in kind,
A frantic toy, a man may easily find.

For who would mark sometime the frantic fits,
The frisks and turns, with tricks in sundry sorts
Would think a dancer quite out of his wits
So to devise to make such skipping sports,
To throw himself about house here and there
As one half mad, who well could rest nowhere.

But to be short, as once I said before,
I say again, Dancing is but a toy,
A skipping sport, which bruiseth bones so sore,
As yields the mind sometime but little joy:
Yet used aright gives cause of great delight,
But yet the best it worketh some despite.

But leaving Dancing, and to Leaping now.
In which some men do not a little joy:
Would such as leap, consider well but how
Their leaping breeds both limbs' and heart's annoy.
Sure they would say, before their legs be burst:
Of all odd sports, yet Leaping is the worst.

LEAPING, THE EIGHTH PLEASURE.

Some men leap short and fall into a ditch,
And who leaps so is laughed at for his pain:
Some men in leap their legs give such a twitch
As ten to one if ere they leap again.
Some their legs slip, and fall upon their back
And think what pain if once the chin-bone[108] crack.

Some when they slip they fall upon their arm,
And some upon their head, and that's the worst:
And who falls so may hap to have such harm
That he may well think leaping sport accursed.
And he that leaps most lightly of them all
Shall have great hap and if he miss a fall.

And he that takes in pleasure such delight
As seeks thereby the prick and praise to gain:
Let him have skill, and be he ne'er so light,
In leaping yet he straineth every vein.
Of which, if once he chance to strain too far,
He may thereby his leaping wholly mar.

Now some again will stumble at a straw
And lightly think to leap over a block:
But who leaps so will prove himself a Daw.[109]
And on his shins perhaps receive a knock.
But now such leaps are meant another way,
And therefore now no more of Leaps I say.

Save only this, that I would wish each one
For to delight, and use his leaping so:
As that he venture not to break a bone
Nor unawares do work himself such woe
As that he find it not to his despite:
Rather a pain then any sweet delight.

WRASTLING, THE NINTH PLEASURE.

And as of leaping, so of wrastling too,
Which with the rest may well be thought a toy:
Yet some do so delight in kind to do,
As that they take in wrastling such a joy,
As for to give their foe a cleanly fall:
They venture will both him and life and all.

And some in wrastling wrest a leg a two,
And some an arm, some back-bone now and than,
And some to break a Wrastler's neck will do
In wrastling oft the best or worst he can.
And is it not a pretty kind of sport,
That breeds delight in such despiteful sort?

What should I need of wrastling more to write?
Who loves the sport, much good do them withal,
For I myself would rather stand upright
Then put my life in venture for a fall.
And he who sets therein his greatest joy,
In time shall find it but a foolish toy.

CLIMBING, THE TENTH PLEASURE.

And as of Leaping, so some men again,
In climbing too do take a great delight,
Which half way up come tumbling down again,
I will not say how much, to their despite.
For commonly, who falleth from a loft,
It is most like he falls not very soft.

The country Clown delights to climb a tree,
And he that climbs the straightest tree of all,
He is the man, Nan will have none but he.
But if in climbing Thomas take a fall,

Then all is marred, and ah poor silly Tom
Hath lost his love, and must go limping home.

And if he scape and get up like a man,
What is his gain, except a nest of Rooks?
And for his pains, he getteth of his Nan
A kindly kiss and two or three sweet looks.
But Sir, and that may prove in time
Enough to make him merely[110] to climb.

Some lusty Simon on a Sunday too
Will climb a May-pole for his Susan's sake:
And on the top will hang a handkirchoo
For him that dare down thence again to take.
But if both he and handkircher fall down,
He likes no more of climbing for a crown.

But leaving louts, some gallant youths delight
In ships by ropes the gallant top to climb:
Who if they hap to miss their climbing right,
They kill a Mariner at the first time,
And get they up, what is it but a toy?
A practise meet but for a desperate boy.

And he again that best of all can scape,
And climbs topgallant, May-pole, or a tree:
Yet for his life he climbs not like an Ape,
And let him climb, he climbs alone for me.
And for my life, when he hath climbed his best,
He thinks himself on ground yet most at rest.

Now some again ungracious grafts[111] sometime,
Both willingly[112], and yet against their will
Do seek the mean three trees at once to climb,
But who climbs so may think his climbing ill.
For by a ladder up they go in haste,
And by a rope they tumble down as fast.

And tell me now, weigh climbing well in mind,
And I believe that you will justly say:
So little is the good that one shall find,
And dangers such in climbing any way.
That he that climbs the cunningest of all
Is many ways yet subject to a fall.

Call but to mind how Phaeton sometime
With willful climbing fell from lofty sky
And brake his neck, how Icarus would climb
With Dedalus, but soaring too too high
To father's grief God wot, as low he fell,
With other mo, that were too long to tell.

Let this suffise, I think it not unmeet
For ship-men's boys, top-gallant for to climb,
And for such clowns as think Rook's flesh is sweet
To climb by leisure such odd trees sometime,
But this I say, to gain a Kaiser's cope,
Climb not three trees, to fall down by a rope.

Besides, I warn each one that hath no skill,
To climb no higher then feet may touch the ground:
Let him climb up, and climb, and climb his fill,
For though he fall, it breeds no deadly wound.
Besides I wish no man to climbing trust,
Nor yet to climb more than of force he must.

For if the clown that climbeth up a tree
A bough do break, and he let slip his hold:
With heave and ho then tumbling down comes he:
And God he knows his pennyworth is cold[113],
For all the Rooks' nests all the town can climb
Makes not amends for his hurt that one time.

Even so in ship the boy that seeks to climb
By cords and lines, if either rope do slip,
Or hand or foot, as many do sometime,

Then down amain he falls into the ship.
Or in the Sea, where hundred then to one
He never scapes; there's one young Sea-man gone.

Yet do I not forbid to climb at all,
For some must climb, and those I well allow:
But yet I wish the best to fear a fall
And those that climb at all, to climb, but how?
When need requires, and then so carefully,
As that they come not down too hastily.

For some must climb, as in assault sometime
Some men of force must seek to scale a Fort:
Then happy he that cunningly can climb
By ropes or ladders, or by any sort
That is, and he of glory gains the crown,
That's soonest up, and latest throwen down.

So then I say, of climbing thus I end,
Who climbeth best finds climbing but a toy:
And I would warn each one I count my friend
For to conceive in climbing little joy.
Least that he find in climbing his delight
By break-neck falls to breed his deadly spite.

And as of climbing, so in Fencing now,
Arts much alike, wherein too many joy:
Which foolish joy doth breed I say to you,
To thousands of your deadly hearts' annoy.
As in my mind, a most accursed sort
To breed delight in such despiteful sport.

FENCING, THE ELEVENTH PLEASURE.

Now sir, this joy in Art of great Defence,
Which of Offence may rather well be named,

Is not obtained without some great expence,
Nor yet without some limb or other lamed
Except by hap you chance to scape the worst,
And yet you part then with your noddle burst,

And let me but demand this question now,
Will you be pleased with him that brake your pate?
Or will you not, almost you care not how,
Seek your revenge, and bear him deadly hate,
Until you be revenged in like sort:
And tell me then, is not this pretty sport?

Perhaps again you have your eye thrust out,
Or catch a scratch cross overthwart[114] your face:
Or else be swaddled[115] roughly round about,
Both shoulders, sides, arms, legs, and every place.
At parting now, Sir, when you feel the smart:
Will you not think Fencing a joyful Art?

By Fencing grows our terms of the Bravado[116],
Our foins[117] and thrusts, the deadly stab and all:
Which some more finely call a Stabbado[118],
And some a blow, a cleanly wipe[119] do call;
And some a rake[120], that crosseth both the shins,
Now with such stuff this joyful sport begins.

Lie here, lie there, strike out your blow at length,
Strike and thrust with him, look to your dagger hand:
Believe me sir, you bear a gallant strength,
But choose your ground, at vantage where to stand,
And keep a loofe[121] for catching too much harm:
Beware the button of your Buckler arm.

With other terms that were too long to tell,
Besides, myself have small skill in that art,
But this I wot, unto my cost too well,
A waster's[122] end hath made my shoulders smart.
And when by chance I caught a smoking[123] blow,

I put it up, or take two or three moe.

And sure I think, who doth indeed delight
To follow Fencing, as some swashers[124] do:
Shall be thereby so boldened for to fight
As willful end in time will bring them to.
Except that God do give them grace indeed
To use their art but in defence at need.

And uséd so, it will not do amiss,
And so I think some skill is requisite:
But I cannot like very well of this,
That any man should so therein delight
As he should set therein so great a joy,
As many do, unto their great annoy.

What should I need of Fencing more to write?
Well used I think it is a pretty art:
But by your leave, who doth therein delight
Shall buy his pleasure with his body's smart.
And so I end, use it to save your life:
But let it not make you to live in strife.

And then in God's name, use it at your will,
So that you use it to your own defence:
But if in fight you chance your foe to kill,
His death will sure abide your conscience.
Yet for all that use it but to defend:
And learn the arts, it will not much offend.

But as I said before, I say again,
Learn it, but love it not in any wise:
Least little pleasure breed your pain[125],
By hurt, by maim, or deadly jeopardies.
And think it but an art of small delight,
Which many ways doth work full great despite.

But leaving now of Fencing more to write,

There is as now another kind of joy:
Wherein some men do take so great delight
As that in time it breeds their great annoy,
They toil themselves, and thrift they throw away,
And lame their legs to learn a foolish play.

TENNIS, THE TWELFTH PLEASURE.

What sport is it to cut[126] a Ball in kind[127],
Or strike a Ball into the hazard[128] fine
Or bandy[129] Balls, to fly against the wind,
Or strike a ball low level o'er the line,
Or make a Chase[130] or hazard[131] for a game,
Then with a brickle wall[132] to win the same.

Oh brave delights, but he that thinks upon
The unknown charge that groweth by the same
Will say, when once his store of coin is gone,
Of all sports Tennis is a costly game.
Which cost considered, soon will drive away
The dear delight that grows by Tennis play.

Yet will I not dispraise the Tennis so
That I would wish no man should use the same.
For by the game no hurt is like to grow,
Except a man do too much use the same.
For I would have it used for exercise:
In some cold mornings, and not otherwise.

For as I said in other things before,
'Tis not the thing, but the delight therein
That makes or mars, delights or grieveth sore,
Then take good heed when first you do begin.
To take delight in any kind of thing:
For too much joy doth after sorrow bring.

Then use the Tennis wisely now and than,

To exercise your lustless limbs withal:
And do not think to do more then you can
With labouring and toiling at a ball,
Lest that you think, instead of sweet delight,
With painful toil you buy a dear despite.

And as of Tennis, so again I find
In other sports, as shooting, bowling too:
Wherein too many so much set their mind
As all day long they little else can do.
Would they but weigh the woes thereby they win:
And they would leave their fond delight therein.

SHOOTING, THE THIRTEENTH PLEASURE.

What sport it is to see an arrow fly,
A gallant archer cleanly draw his bow,
In shooting off, again how cunningly
He hath his loose in letting of it go,
To nock it sure, and draw[133] it to the head,
And then fly out, hold straight, and strike it dead,

With other terms that Archers long have used,
As blow wind, stoop, ah, down the wind a bow:
Tush, says another, he may be excused,
Since the last mark, the wind doth greater grow.
At last he claps in the white suddenly,
Then 'Oh well shot' the standers by do cry.

And that one shot is even enough to make
Him sell his coat for store of bow and shafts,
The cost whereof will make his heart to ache
And make him draw but few delightful drafts.[134]
Therefore say I, in shooting the delight
Doth likewise breed with pleasure some despite.

I do not speak particularly of all

The harms that hap unto an archer's purse:
As bow may break, string crack, and feathers fall,
With other haps that makes them swear and curse.
As when sometime there rains a sudden shower,
That bow and shafts may mar all in an hour.

Therefore use shooting as an exercise
To pass the time, but love it not too much:
Lest with the sport you find the costly price
Do make your heart such dear delights to grutch.
Therefore use it but as a pretty toy:
To pass the day, but count it not a joy.

BOWLING, THE FOURTEENTH PLEASURE.

And now to Bowls, a pretty kind of sport.
Wherein so many take so great delight:
That every day such numbers do resort.
To bowling Alleys, that both day and night,
If light would serve they would not be away,
But waste their wealth upon that foolish play.

How some delight to see a round Bowl[135] run
Smoothly away, until he catch a rub:[136]
Then hold thy bias[137], if that cast were won,
The game were up as sure then as a club[138].
Then upright Bowls, that need not any bank,[139]
And for a game a fine throw in the crank.[140]

But if they marked their money run away,
Their coin to cross quite bias from their purse:
'Twould make them leave that costly kind of play,
And liking take in bowling sport the worse.
And yet the sport well used will yield delight:
But love it not, for then it breeds despite.

For joy in games to other kind of joys,

Wherein some men their chief delight repose:
Which weighed well, may well be thought but toys,
Wherein both cost and labour eke we lose.
As Fishing, Fowling, and such like delights:
Which some do love to follow days and nights.

But lo, behold, what great delight we find
In Fishing first, in diverse sundry sorts:
With Nets, and Angles,[141] Weels,[142] and other kind
Of pretty gins,[143] which yield delightful sports.
And with the sports, let's see the spite withal
That oftentimes in Fishing doth befall.

FISHING, THE FIFTEENTH PLEASURE.

Some take delight with Angle for to stand
Near half a day to catch a Pickerel:
And standing so with Angle in his hand,
Perhaps he takes a paltry Shotterel[144].
That what a man hath taken with such pain,
He straight would throw into the brook again.

Some with a worm do angle for an Eel,
Some for a Carpe do angle with a Snail:
But if the hook do catch within a Weel[145],
Then must of force the fisher's cunning fail.
For lose the hook and fray[146] thy fish away,
And stand again without a bite all day.

And is it not a weary kind of sport
To angle all day for a foolish dish:
And lose the hook in such despiteful sort,
And that perhaps or ere you catch a fish.
Me thinks it should be such a foul despite,
As I should take in angling no delight.

Some for a Trout will angle with a fly,

Some for a Roche[147] a gentil[148] make their bait:
Some make their Flies of colours cunningly,
Of silk and hair, a pretty fine deceit
For foolish fish, and yet 'tis but a toy,
Unworthy far for to be thought a joy.

And yet some men do so herein delight,
As in the making of these foolish flies,
They will attend their work both day and night,
And in the morning up betimes arise.
And to the brook, and angle there all day,
And yet perhaps come empty hand away.

Then judge what spite the Fisher doth abide
To lose his pains, and yet receive no sport:
If I said naught, yet some that well have tried
The like themselves, and fished in like sort,
Would say with me, it is a spiteful toy,
Which with much grief doth yield but little joy.

Some love to fish with trammel,[149] drags, bow nets,
With casting nets, and nets of other sorts:
Wherein some man his pleasure wholly sets,
And greatly cares not for no other sports.
But let him look he do not play the fool,
That with his Net, he fling into the pool.

And he that dredgeth like a water dog,
And wades to knees to catch a dish of fish:
And in the end doth draw up but a frog,
Is not he well at ease with such a dish?
Who would not be a Fisherman to gain
Such dainty morsels to requite his pain?

Perhaps again with wading well all day
He catch such cold as sickness do ensue:
An Ague then will make him shaking say,
'Too late (alas) my fond delight I rue.

This wading sport doth yield so great annoy
As that I find in Fishing little joy.'

Now some again besides their labour lost,
And falling sick with catching cold by wet:
By meshes[150] break, may hap to be at cost,
For Lines, and Corks, and mending of the Net,
And that day's work, the mending be so dear,
As fishing scarce will pay for in a year.

What should I say of Fishing more than this,
Fishing used well may seem a pretty sport:
But no delight but may be used amiss,
Then take delight in fishing in such sort:
As that it prove not too much to your cost:
Nor yet lament your labour too much lost.

For Fishing sport I can not justly blame,
If it be uséd as it ought to be:
But such delight as some have in the same,
I cannot choose but blame whenas I see
Some sick, some drowned, with following the joy
They do conceive in such a foolish toy.

And as of fishing, so again I find
In Fowling to the joy that some conceive:
Would some that Fowl but wisely weigh in mind,
And they should soon their oversights perceive.
When they esteem those things delightful joys,
Which as they use, do prove despiteful toys.

FOWLING, THE SIXTEENTH PLEASURE.

Some men will toil in water, frost and snow,
To set a Limetwig for a foolish Snite:[151]
And glad for cold his fingers' ends to blow,
And so stand plodding all day long till night.

And for wild Fowl even like a peaking[152] mome[153]
To catch a Snipe, and bear a tame fool home.

Now some again go stalking with a Gun
To kill a Herne, a Shov'lard[154] or a Crane:
Who plodding so, ere fowling time be done,
Do miss the Fowl, and breed their sudden bane.
As if the piece[155] should break in cracks or flaws,
Or else recoil, and strike a two his jaws.

Or else the wind may hap to blow the fire
Upon his face, and mar his visage quite:
Then tell me now what he would not desire
To go a Fowling for such sweet delight.
Tush, many more such mischiefs do I know,
Which Fowlers find, but were too long to show.

But lest that some should count me for a fool
For to dispraise the sport in Fowling quite:
I say no more, but fall not in the pool
Catch not a Snipe, in setting for a Snite.[156]
Look to the Piece, keep thy face from the fire,
And Fowl in God's name to thine own desire.

But love it not too much, but as it is
Esteem it so, a hard cold sport indeed,
Which used aright, is pleasant, but amiss,
Yields diverse griefs, therefore no more the need.
Follow the sport, nor take therein delight:
Too much I mean, least it do work thee spite.

And thus I leave to speak more of such sports
As with delight do breed as great despite,
And of delights in other sundry sorts
That daily grow, I mean my mind to write.
Which weighéd well are all but foolish toys:
Which with great griefs do yield but little joys.

STUDIES, THE SEVENTEENTH PLEASURE.

Some men delight all day to break their brain
With study strange, as some will spend their time:
In Physic, Law, and some will take great pain
In Music's art, and some will seek to climb
The skies by study in Astronomy:
Some compass countries by Cosmography.

Some men great pains in Necromancy[157] take,
Some love to study Physiognomy:
Which studies make both brains and heart to ache,
And maketh many stark mad ere they die.
Some love to be thought good Palmisters,
And thousands seek to be Philosophers.

Some love to study most Arithmetic,
In Logic some do daily beat their brain:
 And some delight as much in Rhetoric,
And some do joy in histories again.
But very few do take delight indeed
To study that whereof they most have need.

By which who loves shall find a heavenly joy,
A joy besides that never will decay:
And with the joy yields no jot of annoy,
But teacheth us to Heaven the ready way.
Which study is Divinity by name:
God grant us all to study well the same.

PHYSIC THE EIGHTEENTH PLEASURE.

In Physic's art, let's see what joy we find,
We heal the sick by Medicines we make:
By virtues rare, of herbs of sundry kind,
By waters, oils, and how we ought to take
Each in his kind, how best it may prevail:
This Physic's art doth shew for our avail.

But if the man that is of greatest skill
Have not great care in using of this art:
May minister a medicine to kill,
When as he thinks to ease the sick man's smart.
And who doth so may think himself accursed
And Physic count of studies all the worst.

But he that takes such care in each respect
And fears the worst, and seeks to do his best,
Regards the cause, doth not the time neglect,
But wisely works to breed his patient's rest.
In Physic's art well hath he taken pain:
God's favour and good Fame shall be his gain.

But if he so be settled in that art,
And that he count that study for his joy
How best to seek to ease the body's smart,
And seek no medicine for the soul's annoy
When that himself in fine of force must die?
Oh then where shall his soul for comfort cry?

Let him have spent some time in sacred writ,
And in that study set his chief delight,
And he shall there soon find a medicine fit,
To salve and save his soul from peril quite.
Oh blessed study, that doth shew relief
To soul and body in their greatest grief.

In holy writ we learn how to lament
Our sinful life, wherewith we God offend:
There we are taught our sins for to repent
And there we learn how soon we may amend.
There do we read that God must be the mean
To cleanse our souls from all offences clean.

There do we find that penitence procures
Pardon of God, with pardon, pity too:

Which pity sends such comfort as soon cures
The greatest hurt that worldly woes can do.
And there we find God's mercy yields at last
The joys of Heaven, when worldly woes are past.

If Physic then may yield so great delight
For teaching us to save the body's smart,
The study then that soul and body quite
Rids of all woe, doth it not pass all art?
Yes out of doubt, that yields the only joys,
To which compared all studies are but toys.

Then study Physic for necessity,
To heal a hurt, or ease the sick man's smart:
But let thy joy be in Divinity,
Which weighéd well excelleth every art.
For Physic serves but for the body's grief,
Divinity doth yield the soul's relief.

LAW, THE NINETEENTH PLEASURE.

And leaving thus of Physic more to write,
Let's see what joy in study of the Law,
Some men thereby perhaps do take delight
To make wrong right, and right not worth a straw.
Which yields God knows, the poor man's great despite
To be by wrong bereaved of his right.

And when perhaps the Lawyer calls to mind
The wrong so wrought, and weighs the poor man's case,
He doth in time within his conscience find
Such great unrest, as resteth in no place.
And think you then by Law what grievous joy,
Which breedeth so the secret heart's annoy.

Yet will I not so much dispraise the Law
That I would wish no man to like the same:

For then I might be counted well a Daw,
But this I say, who seeks himself to frame
To study Law, I wish him first of all
To study of Divinity to fall.

There first to learn his study how to use
To learn the Law, thereby his own to keep:
And not as some the study do abuse.
By shifts in Law in others' rights to creep
And so by wrong to purchase worldly wealth,
As that it prove a hurt to his soul's health.

Then first peruse the sacred Laws of God,
How he doth will that we our Laws should use,
And justly how he scourgeth with his rod
All such as scorn or else his Laws refuse.
And then to Law to learn to keep thy right:
And help thy friend, let be thy whole delight.

But in respect of holy Laws I say,
Account our studies in the Laws but toys:
When scripture shows the only ready way
For to attain to everlasting joys.
Let then I say, Divinity be thought
The only joy, to which the best is nought.

ASTRONOMY AND PHYSIOGNOMY. THE TWENTIETH PLEASURE.

So could I write too of Astronomy,
By which we climb into the lofty sky:
And so again of Physiognomy,
Whereby by face we wonders do descry,
Divinity heaves us above the sky[158]
And doth to us the power of God descry.

COSMOGRAPHY, AND PHILOSOPHY, THE ONE AND TWENTIETH PLEASURE.

Now see the joy got by Cosmography,
We compass countries learnedly by art:
And what delight by fine Philosophy
By reason strange to prove on either part
False judgement true, and further to descry
Secrets in nature by Philosophy.

By holy writ the way to Heaven we find,
A country far above the lofty sky:
By sacred Laws we can confute in kind
The unjust cause and prove the contrary.
By Scriptures eke God's nature plain we find:
Just, merciful, and to his servants kind.

Now see how far this study doth surpass
All studies else, what so without respect:
Then may he be justly thought an ass,
Which doth this study anything neglect
And counteth not all other studies toys,
Compared to this, which yieldeth heavenly joys.

MUSIC, THE [TWO AND] TWENTIETH PLEASURE.

In Music now a great delight we find,
And sure it is a pretty kind of art:
But oh that we would settle once our mind
To tune our tongues, with sound of humble heart
To sing due laud unto the Lord on high:
Oh that would seem an heavenly harmony.

And now the joys got by Arithmetic,
To number much within a little time:
And some do love to roll in Rhetoric,

Some best like prose, and some delight in Rhyme.
And yet all these considered well in mind,
But trifling toys the true Divine doth find.

DIVINITY, THE TWENTY-THIRD PLEASURE.

Divinity doth number out our days,
And shows our life, still fading as a flower:
Bids us beware of wanton wicked ways,
For we are sure to live no certain hour.
Arithmetic doth number worldly toys,
Divinity innumerable joys.

Then judge I pray which yields the more delight,
Divinity, then choose it for thy joy:
Study that chief, and labour day and night,
By that to learn to shield thee from annoy,
And thou shalt find it salveth every sore
And saves the soul, and what joy can be more?

By Rhetoric, now some do take delight,
To paint a fable with a gallant glose:
But no such tale is grateful in God's sight,
Besides, he will each secret shift disclose.
His tale is best before the Lord who says
He doth in heart repent his sinful days,

Who doth indeed his sinful life confess,
Who pardon craves, and calls to God for grace,
His tale is heard, him God doth rightly bless,
And eke in Heaven provides for him a place.
God grant us all our prayers so to use
That he may not our penitence refuse.

Now some again delight in Histories,
To read the Acts of some courageous Knight,
To think upon the gallant victories,

To read again the order of the fight.
And do such stories breed delight indeed?
Then take delight the Scriptures for to read.

There shalt thou find how Christ a battle fought
Against the devil and his cursed train,
Subdued them all, their force prevailed nought,
But all were driven into eternal pain.
Blessed be he that so hath brought in thrall
Him that would else have surely slain us all.

And tell me then, although some valiant Knight
Did conquer Realms, and by his force of arms
Subduéd Princes by his only might
And made them know his force unto their harms,
Yet think of him that by his only might
Did save both thee, and all the world by fight.

Oh valiant act, and worthy to be read,
Who saved our lives, who else had sure been slain,
And further when our bodies here be dead,
Hath saved our souls from everlasting pain.
God grant us all under that Christ to fight,
Who so our souls hath savéd by his might.

And of good deeds to read dost thou delight
That worthy are for to be borne in mind,
Then read how Christ unto the blind gave sight,
Healéd the sick in body and in mind,
Did give the lame their limbs, and what else more?
Gave the diseased a salve for every sore.

Where can you read of one so good a man?
Tush, there is none without exception:
Let us delight our selves there now and than
His great good deeds to read and look upon,
And we shall find thereby such heavenly joys
As we shall count all Stories else but toys.

For if we do to mind his goodness call,
How great a good he hath bestowed on us,
By his dear death and blood to save us all,
Are we not bound to think only Jesus
To be indeed the Author of our joy,
And only he that keeps us from annoy?

Yes out of doubt, and therefore thus I end,
God grant us all to take him for our joy:
To love our God, which is our only friend,
That saves our souls and bodies from annoy.
And to esteem all worldly things but toys:
And set in Christ our all and only joys.

FINIS.

"THE PAINE OF PLEASURE":A TRANSCRIPTION OF THE ORIGINAL TEXT (1580)

This text is transcribed from the copy of "The Paine of Pleasure" now in the British Library. The unique original title page of the collection, now in the Pepysian Library, Cambridge, is reproduced below.

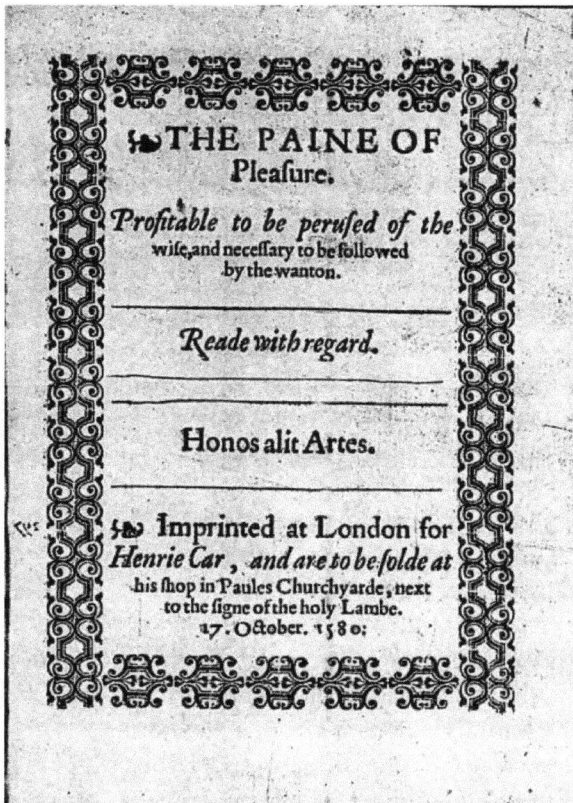

THE PAINE OF Pleafure.

Profitable to be perufed of the wife, and neceffary to be followed by the wanton.

Reade with regard.

Honos alit Artes.

Imprinted at London for Henrie Car, and are to be folde at his fhop in Paules Churchyarde, next to the figne of the holy Lambe.
17. October. 1580.

When I sometime begin to weigh in minde
The wretched state of miserable man:
Me thinkes (alas) I presently doe finde,
Such suddaine harmes that happen now & than.
  As euerie way doe plainely séeme to show:
  That man dooth liue within a world of woe.
¶For first in birth we worke our mothers woe,
In infancie we cause our Parents care:
In further péeres, we fall in miserie,
From vertues line, and light in sinfull snare.
  In further péeres, we wander too and fro,
  And last in age, God knoweth howe we die.
¶ In childish péeres, we first with cries begin,
To shew in age, such sorrowes as ensue:
In lustie youth, we dayly trauaile in
Such wicked wayes, as wicked age dooth rue.
  In such a sorte, our elder péeres we spend:
  As in our age, doe bréede our dolefull end.
¶ And for the ioyes that in our life we finde,
Which are but few, and yet not frée from woe:
What are they all, but Feathers in the winde
Which euery tempest tosseth too and fro.
  Which tempests so, are rising euery day:
  As in short space blow all our ioyes away.
¶ And now such ioyes, as we short time enioy,
From tender péeres, euen till our dying howre:
Which many wayes are mixed with annoy,
So that each swéete, dooth yéeld as sharpe a sowre.
  Marke what they be, as I doe shew them plaine,
  And you may sée, eache pleasures fruite is paine.
¶ In infancie, what is our chiefest ioy?

The Nurſes dug, whoſe milke may marre the Childe:
And then delight in many a gaudie toy,
Whoſe gariſh hue, doth make our wits ſo wilde.
     As in ſuch ſorte dooth ſettle our delight:
     As doth our wits withdrawe from wiſdome quite,
¶ Then to be dandled in our mothers lappe,
And to be ſtrokt at cockring Fathers hand:
When better were by now and then a rappe.
For to be kept in true obedience band.
     Then to be cockte of both our Parents ſo:
     As that in yéeres it turne vnto our woe.
¶ For Mothers milde, that thinke they loue the child,
By kéeping him from Fathers crueltie:
In time of yéeres, may finde her ſelfe beguild,
By letting him haue lauiſh libertie.
     For libertie in youth, dooth run ſuch race:
     As quite forgets the path of perfect grace.
¶ And then (alas) too late comes had I wiſt,
And then they blame the nature of the Childe:
Which they might well haue bridled as they liſt,
But wantonnes hath made the wits ſo wilde.
     As rather runnes in vale of vanitie:
     Then ſéekes the pathe of perfect pietie.
¶ But let me leaue to ſpeake of childiſh yéeres,
And let me write of luſtie gallant youth:
Who through the world doth trauaile with his péers
Such wayes in age, as moues his minde to ruth.
     And in ſuch toyes doth ſet his chiefe delight,
     As that in age dooth worke his vtter ſpight.

Beautie, The firſt pleaſure.

For now beholde in youth, one chiefeſt ioy,
  In which too many, moſt delight doe finde:
Which though well waide, is but in déede a toy,
Yet to delight, allures the wiſeſt minde.
     Which thing to name, is Beauties heauenly hue:
     Which yéeldes delight, that thouſands dayly rue.
¶ For beautie firſt bréedes liking in the minde,
Liking bréedes luſt, luſt lewdnes, lewdnes, what:
Such world of woes, as age doth quickly finde,

And cries (alas) repentance all too late.
      Sée beautie then, in youth the chiefest ioy,
      In age is séene to worke no small annoy.
¶ Beautie in some doth cause a kinde of pride,
And pride must be maintained all by cost:
And cost makes youth, in age his head to hide,
 For shame or debt, when all his wealth is lost.
      But oh fond youth to ioy in Beautie so:
      As that in age his ioy doth bréede such woe.
¶ In other some, yet Beautie worketh woorse,
It makes accesse, of such as practise ill:
Whose ill accesse the beautifull may curse,
That vnto vice allure their wanton will.
      Oh vile delight, where Beautie so is plast:
      To make in déede, the fairest face disgrast.
¶ In some againe it bréedes a great delight,
In modest mindes, whose heartes are not at rest:
But thousand pangs, are dayly forst to proue,
 For louing them, whome beautie so hath blest.
      For lucklesse lots, so follow louers ioy:
      As many wayes doth worke them great annoy.
¶ But where the face, with beautie is bedeckt,
And beares withall a modest countenance:
Whose minde againe to vertue hath respect,
And thereby séekes, their state for to aduaunce.
      There will I say it is no foolish toy:
      But thought in déede a rare and heauenly ioy.
¶ But to be short, in youth our chiefe delight,
As first I said, in beauties heauenly hue:
As well in youth as age, worke such despight,
As well may make the stoutest hart to rue,
      Which now I leaue, and to some other toy:
      Which yéeldes great woe, but to a little ioy.

Riches. The second pleasure.

In Ritches now, another kinde of ioy,
  In which both youth and age haue great delight:
Were it well waide, and it were but a toy,
Which manie waies doe bréede their great despight.

In getting firſt with labour, care and paine,
In kéeping to, as great vnreſt againe.
¶ In getting firſt, the braine is buſied,
With déepe deuiſe to caſt a plot to gaine:
Then armes, hands, legges and féete, are occupied,
For cankered coyne, their ſtrongeſt ioynt to ſtraine
I doe not meane, as ſome vnwiſely doe:
Deuiſe for coyne, to ſtraine a necke ioynt too:
¶ God forbid that, and yet ſome men doe ſo,
Both ſtretch and cracke, and breake their necke ioynt to:
But wealth ſo wunne. dooth bréede no little woe,
God mend their mindes that ſo deuiſe to doe.
Better to die a begger of the twaine:
Then by ſuch meanes to ſéeke or gape for gaine.
¶ This is (alas) a wicked way to gaine:
Yet not the wurſt: for ſome, oh curſed they:
That ſéeke the meane to haue their parents ſlaine,
And Friendes and kinſfolkes, cloſely make away.
To gaine their goods, but oh ill gotten gaine:
Whoſe getting bréedes, the ſoule eternall paine.
¶ God ſhield each one, from ſuch a beaſtly thought,
So to deuiſe, to purchaſe worldly pray:
And pardon thoſe that wickedly haue wrought,
Such deuilliſh meanes to worke their ſoules decay.
And graunt vs all ſo for to ſéeke for wealth:
As neckes cracke not, nor hinder our ſoules health.
¶ But leauing theſe, lets ſée ſome other waies,
In making meanes, to hoorde vp heapes of pence:
In ſtrange deuiſe, to ſpend both night and dayes,
And leaue their home, and goe a great way hence.
To find ſuch ſtuffe, as to returne againe:
Doo yéeld them ſmall amends for all their paine.
¶ Some ſaile by ſea, to ſéek out forraine ſoyle,
To finde out there ſome gem, of vaur great.
In ſéeking which, with tough and tedious toyle,
To ſaue themſelues, they oft ar faine to ſweat.
And ere their Barks, be ſafe ariu'd on land
How oft their liues in thouſand dangers ſtand.
¶ And let their ſhips be ſafely ſet on ſhore,
And they do finde, that which they looke for there:
Yet ere returne, they liue perplexed ſore,
With troubled minde, now ſayling halfe in feare.

Of forraine foes. of tempeſts, Rocks, or Sands:
Or falling into rouing Pirats hands.
¶ And let them be returned home with ioy,
And all their goods brought home to their deſire:
Yet ſée what then doth worke their harts annoy,
Oh then they feare each fooliſh ſparke of fire,
Should burne their houſe, and then another gréefe,
Each Mouſe that péepes, ſhould ſurely be a théefe.
¶ Some other now, that loue to liue at home,
And onely ſéeke by ſweat of brow to gaine:
With ſpade and ſholue about the fieldes they rome,
Turmoyling ſtill with labour ſore and paine.
With carke and care, to purchaſe wealth in haſt:
Which God he knowes, but little time will laſt.
¶ Some ſéeke by play, at Tables, Cardes, and Dice,
In ſecret ſort, a world of wealth to winne:
But who ſéeke ſo, doe proue themſelues vnwiſe,
In looſing all, before their gaine beginne.
Whoſe hope of gaine can neuer bréede ſuch ioy,
As certaine loſſe, doth bréede their harts annoy.
¶ What ſhould I write of euery ſtrange deuiſe,
That ſome men vſe in ſéeking worldly pelfe:
The prouerbe ſaies, that no man can be wiſe,
That is not wiſe each way to helpe himſelfe.
But ſcripture ſayes, the rich to Heauen on high
Goes like a Cammell, through a Néedles eye.
¶ And let a man grow rich in luſty youth,
And haue for wealth almoſt the world at will,
Yet ſée in age, God wot too great a ruth,
It bréedeth death full ſore againſt their will.
How ioyes he then? in being his owne friend:
To bring his life, his chiefeſt ioy to end.
¶ O fond delight, oh grieuous kinde of ioy
Oh cankred coyne, the cauſe of deadly paine:
Oh madhead man to ioy in ſuch a toy,
Oh gréedie mindes that ſo doe grope for gaine.
Oh wretched wealth, whoſe ioy dooth bréede ſuch wo,
Oh God forgiue ſuch fooles as ſéeke it ſo.
¶ But let wealth paſſe, one other ioy I finde,
Which many count their great and chiefeſt ioy,
Which if they would once wiſely way in minde,
They ſoone ſhould ſée it plainely but a toy.

Which when God wot with great a doe they gaine,
Yet being got, it is not frée from paine.

Honour, The third pleafure.

Which ioy to tell, by name is Honour hie,
    Which nobleſt mindes account the greateſt ioy:
Which firſt obtainde, by deadly ieopardie,
They doe God knowes, with care enough enioy.
    Oh man moſt madde to loue ſo vaine a thing,
    As with ſmall ioy, doth thouſand ſorrowes bring.
¶ Loe, firſt the care in ſéeking how to clime,
With ſtudie ſtrange, how it doth beate our braine:
In climing then our obſeruaunce of time,
Then héede to holde, leaſt we goe downe againe.
    The feare to fall, and if we fall, what then?
    But feare of death, which happes to many men.
¶ Let vs ſcape death, yet may we breake a bone,
Or lame a limme, or bruſe vs inwardly:
Or catch a clap may make our harts to grone,
And bréede our death, although not preſently.
    Let vs miſſe theſe, and haue no harme at all:
    Yet will it be a griefe to take a fall.
¶ And if againe, they venter for to clime,
Then muſt they be more warie then before:
For if they chaunce to fall the ſecond time,
Tis ten to one but they are bruſed ſore.
    Yet if they liue, and ſéeke to clime againe,
    And third time fall, that brings a deadly paine.
¶ Now ſundry men, deuiſe a ſundry meane,
To make their way to Honour to attaine:
What two will chuſe, the third miſliketh cleane,
And glory ſéekes another way to gaine.
    But he that ſéekes the beſt way that he can:
    Shall finde vnſought ſome ſorrow now and then.
¶ And now and then, ſuch ſorrowes as in déede,
If euery man would wiſely way in minde,
We ſoone ſhould ſée, how farre they doe excéede,
The little ioyes that we by honour finde.
    Oh minde moſt vaine, to ſéeke ſo vaine a ioy:
    Which many wayes doth worke ſo great annoy.

¶ And now, as men doe sundry meanes deuise,
To scale the toppe of Honours stately throne:
So doe their sorrowes diuers wayes arise,
Which makes their mindes, to make a sundry mone.
     Some sigh and sob in secrete sorte alone:
      To make their griefe, vnto the world vnknowne.

¶ For loe, some men doe seeke, by force of armes,
To gaine the honour of a valiant Knight:
Which by ill hap vnto their dayly harmes,
Doe finde a foe to vanquish them in fight.
     In seeking then to clime to Honour so,
      Or death or maime doth breede their deadly woe.

¶ Some other seeke by Riches to attaine,
Euen in the top of Honour high to sit:
But climing vp, Fates sling them downe againe,
As men in deede for such a place vnfit.
     Which if they fall, and riches fall withall:
      Way then what griefe doth fret them at the gall.

¶ Some fondly thinke, by wasting wealth to gaine,
The honour due to liberality:
Which contrary vnto their pinching paine,
Get the dispraise of prodigality.
     Which when (alas) their wealth is gone and spent,
      Oh thinke how then their follies they lament.

¶ But let these men that seeke for honour so,
As first the Knight that seekes by force of armes
T'obtaine the same, yet see his after woe,
In midst of ioy, vnto his deadly harmes
     Another comes that is of greater might:
      And dispossesse him of his honour quite.

¶ Oh then by losse the griefe doth farre exceede
His little ioy in keeping of the same:
Euen so the Churle that by his pence indeede,
May win a while, the Forte of noble fame.
     Yet vnawares such fortune may befall,
      That he may loose, both Honour, coyne and all.

¶ And then what griefe the couetous conceiue,
By losse of coyne their great and chiefest ioy:
A man that hath but one eie may perceiue,
That nothing more can breede their harts annoy.
     And though their griefe of honour lost be least,
      Yet who would part with honour once possest?

¶ Now they that do by spending frée obtaine,
Of many men, perhaps a noble name:
Yet noble mindes can finde no greater paine,
Then want of wealth for to maintaine the same.
       Whose falling so, doth worke them much despight,
       As doth their harts bereaue of all delight.
¶ But who would séeke the perfect way to clime,
To Honours throne, and surely there to sit:
Must wisely séeke with obseruance of time,
By Uertues line the ready way to hit.
       For Uertue gaines, in life a noble name:
       And after death immortall noble Fame.
¶ Uertue is it, that onely yéeldeth ioy,
A ioy besides that euer will endure:
And such a ioy as worketh no annoy,
But doth indéede a heauenly ioy procure.
       Oh ioy of ioyes, by thée God graunt vs all:
       To clime to heauen, and neuer thence to fall.
¶ But let me leaue of Honour now to write,
And speake my minde of meaner kinde of ioyes:
Which to some mindes do giue a great delight,
Yet wisely waide, are nothing else but toyes.
       And with their ioyes, which are but small indéede,
       What woes they worke, which farre their ioyes excéede.

Loue, The fourth pleasure.

Of little ioyes, behold this first for one,
  Some, Ladies loue do count a heauenly ioy:
In séeking which, some are so woe begone,
As harts consume with griefe and great annoy.
       And some haue bene in loue so ouer shooes,
       As lacke or losse, makes them their liues to loose.
¶ For sundry men, by sundry meanes do séeke,
Their Ladies loue or liking to procure,
And what they thinke, that may their fancies kéepe,
That must they doe, what paine they so endure.
       What gem so rare, may please their mistresse eye:
       Cost lands and life, but Louers dayly buy.
¶ And let wealth waste, then loue begins to shrinke,
And when loue shrinkes, then farewell louers ioy:

Then wretched wightes, in sorrow so must sincke,
And worthy well to ioy in such a toy.
  As so to séeke, and labour day by day,
   To purchase that dooth bréede their owne decay.
¶ Sée then by loue, what cost, what care, what woe?
In getting first, and kéeping then with paine:
In getting first, what dayly griefes doe grow,
In loosing then, what more despight againe.
   Oh madhead man, to ioy in such a thing:
   And with small ioy, doth thousand sorrowes bring.

Horses, *Hawkes*, and *Dogs*, The fift Pleasure

A nd so I leaue to write of Louers ioy,
 Which many wayes doth worke a world of woe:
And I will now speake of some other ioy,
Which with small ioy, doth diuers sorrowes sowe
  As Horses, hawkes, houndes, birdes of diuers sortes,
  Which to some mindes, doe make delightfull sportes.
¶ As first, behold the stately stamping Stéede,
That snuffes and snorts, and stands vpon no ground,
I must confesse a ioyfull sight in déede,
But he that hath the toyle and labour found,
  In bringing him vnto that passe at first,
  Will thinke of ioyes, the ioy in horse the worst.
¶ Nowe he againe that neuer takes the paine,
To breake him so, but haue him broke to hand,
I thinke in déede, hath more ioy of the twaine,
 In stately sort to sée him stamping stand.
  But if he take delight to ride him too:
  Let him take héede what then hée séekes to doe.
¶ For such a ioy may hap to bréede such woe,
By iollitie in ryding without skill:
That he by fall, may catch so sore a blow,
As downe on ground, may make him lye there still.
  Where broken bones, lim lambde, or bruses sore:
  Will make him ioy in praunsing horse no more.
¶ And if againe he chaunce to sit him fast,
Whereby he may the more increase his ioy:
Yet is hée not assurde his ioy will last,
But it will turne vnto his great annoy.

For by ill hap his horſe may fall ſore ſicke,
Or halt downe right, by ſhooing ill, or pricke.
¶ Perchance againe he ride him till he ſweate,
And ſet him vp vnwalked, ſomewhat hote:
And ſo doo make him catch ſo ſore a heate,
As ten to one if ſhortly he dye not.
      And if he dye, then farewell Maiſters ioy:
      And Ryders paynes, and farewell fooliſh toy.

Hawkes.

So ioy in Hawkes, good Lord how ſome delight,
To ſée them kill a byrd of meaner ſtrength:
Some marke the pitch in making of their flight,
Some loue the Hawke that flyeth out at length.
      Some moſt of all, the ſhort wingde hawke eſtéeme,
      Some long wingde hawkes the braueſt birdes doe déeme.
¶ Some loue to ſée the Goſhawke roughly ruſh,
Thorow the woods, and perch from trée to trée,
And ceaze vpon the Feſant in the buſh,
And ſure it is a prettie ſporte to ſée.
      But in reſpect of any worthy ioy:
      God knowes it is but euen a very toy.
¶ But let it be to ſome a great delight,
Yet ſée what toyle it dayly brings withall:
Firſt, if ſhe take a gadding in her flight,
Then ride and runne, and marre Horſe, man and all.
      And tyre themſelues to ſéeke a fooliſh Kite,
      Yet looſe her too, and then what greater ſpight?
¶ And let her be the fineſt Hawke that is,
And neuer gad, nor haue ill qualities:
And what ſhée flyes at, ſéeld or neuer miſſe,
Yet is ſhée not quite frée from ieopardies.
      Some fooliſh thorne may ſtrike atoo her wing,
      And flying marde, then farewell fooliſh thing.
¶ What ſhould I néede of other Hawkes to write?
As Faulcon, Taſſel, Lanner, and Lanneret:
With little Hawkes, that Ladies take delight
Fine Faulknor like, vpon their fiſt to ſet.
      As Sparhawke, Merline, birds I muſt confeſſe,
      For Ladies fit, I can well ſay no leſſe.
¶ But of all Hawkes, thoſe Hawkes are yet the worſt,

For if they catch a bruse abroade in flight,
Then tender harts, straight into teares they burst,
For loosing of a little péeuish Kite.
      A goodly thing to giue such cause of ioy,
      As béeing lost, should bréede so great annoy.

¶ Now some againe it is a sport to sée,
What mone they make, some first will sighing say:
It is my lucke, what most delighteth mée,
Comes to some mischiefe one or other way.
      And some will say, my froward dreame tonight,
      Pretended me this day some foule dispight.

¶ But let me leaue of Beasts and birds to write,
And let me now vnto some other ioyes:
Which with delight, doe bréede as great dispight,
Which wisely wayde, may well be thought but toyes.
      As dauncing, singing, wrestling, leaping too:
      Which who almost but doeth delight to doo.

¶ Which pleasant sports, ere they be well attainde,
Do bréede some paine, to them that séeke the same:
And some of them ere they be throughly gaind,
Doe often strike some limme or other lame.
      I will not say, though some haue found it so:
      Some of their sports, doe bréede their deadly woe.

Musicke, The sixt pleasure.

But let me first of Musicke speake my minde,
Which with some sport doth yéeld as great a spight,
The little Boy, first by his eares doth finde,
In plaine-song pulles is very small delight.
      In pricke-song then, a priuie pinch or two:
      Makes him in song, haue little minde vnto.

¶ And way the time that wantonly ye spend,
First in the Notes, and then againe in Cliffes:
How to ascend, and then againe descend,
By Larges and Longs, by Bréefes and Semibréefes.
      Minims, Crochets, Quauers, Sharps, Flats, to faine:
      Vt, re, me, fa, sol, la, and backe againe.

¶ Then when you know your notes and how to sing,
Then instruments of Musicke must be had:
And then an eare to euery sundry string,

Which makes some men, my selfe haue séene halfe mad.
>For earnest harkening to the Musicks sound:
>Makes some oft times too farre in Musicke drownd.

¶ And is it not a prettie sport thinke you,
That makes one mad ere he attaine the same?
I take it so, and this belieue me now,
Who séekes himselfe to Musikes arte to frame,
>And very young is set to Musickes schoole,
>In other artes, proues commonly a foole.

¶ It is a sport of troth sometime to sée,
A right Musition in his formall grace:
How he can looke, as if it were not he,
Especially, when that he is in place.
>Whereas he thinkes himselfe to be the best:
>For pride or praise, how he can straine his brest.

¶ But if there come another into place,
Better then he, then downe his feathers fall:
Then Frauncis Fidler, with his formall face,
Shrinketh aside, and gets him next the wall.
>And for a pound, he sings not one Note more,
>Where comes a better then he was before:

¶ But what? me thinkes that some begins to frowne,
To write so much in Fidlers foule dispraise:
Why, if there be some such odde fidling Clowne,
As plaies at Hertford on the Hollidayes:
>And takes the matter so much in disgrace:
>For all his Fidle, fart in his fooles face.

¶ For such Musitions makes some Minions méete,
With their swéete harts on some ungratious gréene:
Where after each hath other friendly gréete,
Somewhat haps else that may not there be séene.
>As bargaines made, that must be gréed upon,
>Behinde some bush, when all the crue is gone.

¶ But let me leaue off lowtish Musicke now,
To write more wordes, and let me somewhat say
Of Courtly Musicke, which I say to you,
I cannot well reproue in any way.
>Although perhaps some wantons thereby finde,
>A time to play the wantons in their kinde.

¶ I meane no harme in that I say in kinde,
For wantonnes and wickednes are two:
Tis not the grace in any, but the minde,

That mooues a man, or good or bad to doe.

    A merry minde a gentle nature ſhowes:

    When ſullen lookes are ſignes of ſurle ſhrowes.

¶ And yet doo ſome perhaps, in dauncing déeme,

That Louers then haue time of great delight,

But if two loue one Lady, it muſt ſéeme,

The ones delight, the others great deſpight.

    And if but one, yet then his preſent ioy:

    May turne in time vnto as great annoy.

¶ For then perhaps he reapes good countenance,

Good wordes, and more, perhaps with all good will:

Beſides, he hath good licence in his Daunce,

Without ſuſpect to looke and talke his fill.

    And to receiue great fauour of his friend,

    Which when his daunce is done, are all at end.

¶ And then (alas) conſider what deſpight

He bides, to thinke vpon his pleaſures paſt:

And ſées againe, his ſwéete and whole delight,

With poſting ſpéede to fade away ſo faſt,

    No greater griefe I thinke can fortune frame:

    Then win delight, and then to looſe the ſame.

Dauncing, The ſeuenth pleaſure.

And touching now the harmes that often hap,

  to ſuch as ſéeke, for to be excellent:

In Dauncing catch ſome time ſo ſore a clap,

By froward falles, as makes them to repent.

    The tumbling tricks, and turning on the toe,

    When leggs doe grow ſo lame they cannot goe.

¶ And ſome braue youthes will labour day and night,

Till they haue got the Caprey, and croſſe poynt:

But tell me now, how much will they delight

When that they ſée they legs croſt out of ioynt:

    Or els perhaps with ſome vntoward fall:

    Then breake their arme, or ſometime necke and all.

¶ Oh then behold, in Dauncing what delight,

Which bréedes the Dauncers oft vntimely end:

And for my ſelfe, I ſée ſuch great deſpight,

By dauncing growe, as he that were my friend,

    Sure I would wiſh him leaue all dauncing quite,

Then in such toyes to take so great delight.
¶ Besides, sometime in dauncing we doe sée,
Quarrels arise, yea, betwixt friend and friend:
Which once begun, God knowes but seldome be
Without great hurt, brought vnto quiet end.
 Consider then the great and dire despight:
 In dauncing growes, in midst of most delight.
¶ What should I néede of dauncing more to write?
First of the paines in learning how to daunce:
And then againe how great and foule despight,
In dauncing oft to many men doth chaunce.
 Let this suffize, it is but euen a toy,
 Whose vse may yéelde a pleasure or annoy.
¶ For least I should séeme to dispraise it quite,
In prayse of dauncing thus much will I say,
Who knowes in déede, how for to vse it right.
May daunce full well, I will not say him nay.
 For so it is an honest exercise:
 And one in déede of Courtly qualities.
¶ But for to set in dauncing such delight,
As it should séeme, to giue great cause of ioy:
Who déemes it so, they are deceiued quite,
For God he knowes, it is but euen a toy.
 And such a toy, as sure estéemde in kinde,
 A franticke toy, a man may easilie finde.
¶ For who would marke sometime the franticke fits,
The frisks and turnes, with trickes in sundry sortes:
Would thinke a Dauncer, quite out of his wits,
So to deuise to make such skipping sportes
 To throw himselfe about house, here and there:
 As one halfe mad, who well could rest no where.
¶ But to be short, as once I said before,
I say againe, Dauncing is but a toy:
A skipping sport, which bruseth bones so sore,
As yéeldes the minde sometime but little ioy:
 Yet vsde a right, giues cause of great delight,
 But yet the best it worketh some despight.
¶ But leauing Dauncing, and to Leaping now.
In which some men doe not a little ioy:
Would such as leape, consider well but how,
Their leaping bréedes, both lims and harts annoy.
 Sure they would say, before their legges be burst:

Of all odde sportes, yet Leaping is the wurst.

Leaping, The eight pleasure.

Some men leape short, and fall into a ditch,
And who leapes so, is laught at for his paine:
Some men in leape, their legges giue such a twitch,
As ten to one if ere they leape againe.
      Some their legs slip, and fall vpon their backe:
      And thinke what paine if once the chine-bone cracke.
¶ Some when they slip they fall vpon their arme,
And some vpon their head, and thats the worst:
And who fals so, may hap to haue such harme,
That he may well thinke leaping sporte accurst.
      And he that leapes most lightly of them all,
      Shall haue great hap and if he misse a fall.
¶ And he that takes in pleasure such delight,
As seekes thereby the pricke and praise to gaine:
Let him haue skill, and be he nere so light,
In leaping yet he straineth euery vaine.
      Of which, if one he chaunce to straine too farre,
      He may thereby his leaping wholy marre.
¶ Now some againe will stumble at a straw,
And lightly thinke to leape ouer a blocke:
But who leapes so, will proue himselfe a Daw,
And on his shinnes perhaps receiue a knocke.
      But now such leapes are meant another way,
      And therefore now no more of Leapes I say.
¶ Saue onely this, that I would wish each one,
For to delight, and vse his leaping so:
As that he venter not to breake a bone,
Nor vnawares, doe worke himselfe such woe,
      As that he finde it not to his despight:
      Rather a paine then any sweete delight.

Wrastling, The ninth pleasure.

And as of leaping, so of wrastling too,
Which with the rest, may well be thought a toy:
Yet some doe so delight in kinde to doe,

As that they take in wraſtling ſuch a ioy,

    As for to giue their foe a cleanly fall:

    They venter will, both him and life and all.

¶ And ſome in wraſtling wreſt a legge a two,

And ſome an arme, ſome backe-bone now and than,

And ſome to breake a Wraſtlers necke, will doe

In wraſtling oft, the beſt or worſt he can.

    And is it not a prettie kinde of ſport,

    That bréedes delight in ſuch deſpightfull ſorte?

¶ What ſhould I néede of wraſtling more to write?

Who loues the ſport, much good doe them withall,

For I my ſelfe would rather ſtand vpright,

Then put my life in venture for a fall.

    And he who ſets therein his greateſt ioy,

    In time ſhall finde it but a fooliſh toy.

Climing, The tenth pleaſure.

And as of Leaping, ſo ſome men againe,

In climing to, do take a great delight,

Which halfe way vp, come tumbling downe againe,

I will not ſay how much, to their deſpight.

    For commonly, who falleth from a loft,

    It is moſt like he falls not very ſoft.

¶ The countrey Clowne, delightes to clime a trée,

And he that climes the ſtraighteſt trée of all,

He is the man, Nan will haue none but he.

But if in climing Thomas take a fall,

    Then all is marde, and ah poore ſillie Tom,

    Hath loſt his loue, and muſt goe limping home.

¶ And if he ſcape and get vp like a man,

What is his gaine, except a neſt of Rookes?

And for his paynes, he getteth of his Nan,

A kindely kiſſe, and two or thrée ſwéete lookes.

    But Sir, and that may proue in time,

    Enough to make him merely to clime.

¶ Some luſty Simon on a ſunday too,

Will clime a May-pole for his Suſans ſake:

And on the top will hang a handkirchoo,

For him that dare, downe thence againe to take.

    But if both he and handkircher fall downe,

He likes no more of climing for a crowne.

¶ But leauing lowtes, some gallant youthes delight,

In ships by ropes the gallant top to clime:

Who if they hap to misse their climing right,

They kill a Marriner at the first time,

    And get they vp, what is it but a toy?

    A practise méete but for a desperate boy.

¶ And he againe that best of all can scape,

And climes top gallant, May-pole, or a trée:

Yet for his life he climbes not like an Ape,

And let him clime, hée climes alone for me.

    And for my life, when he hath climde his best,

    He thinks himselfe on ground yet most at rest.

¶ Now some againe vngracious grafts sometime,

Both willingly, and yet against their will:

Doe séeke the meane, thrée trées at once to clime,

But who climes so may thinke his climing ill.

    For by a ladder vp they go in hast,

    And by a rope they tumble downe as fast.

¶ And tell me now, way climing well in minde,

And I beléeue that you will iustly say:

So little is the good that one shall finde,

And dangers such in climing any way.

    That he that climes the cunningest of all,

    Is many waies yet subiect to a fall.

¶ Call but to minde, how Phaæton sometime,

With willfull climing, fell from lofty sky:

And brake his necke, how Icarus would clime,

With Dedalus, but soring too too hie.

    To fathers griefe God wot, as lowe he fell,

    With other mo, that were too long to tell.

¶ Let this suffise, I thinke it not vnméete,

For ship-mens boyes, top gallant for to clime:

And for such clownes, as thinke Rookes flesh is swéete,

To clime by leasure such odde trées sometime.

    But this I say, to gaine a Keisars cope:

    Clime not thrée trées, to fall downe by a rope.

¶ Besides, I warne each one that hath no skill,

To clime no higher then féete may touch the ground:

Let him clime vp, and clime, and clime his fill,

For though he fall, it bréedes no deadly wound.

    Besides I wish, no man to climing trust:

Nor yet to clime, more then of force he must.
¶ For if the clowne that climeth vp a trée,
A bough doe breake, and he let slip his hold:
With heaue and hoe, then tumbling downe comes he:
And God he knowes his penywoorth is colde.
　　　　For all the Rookes nestes all the towne can clime,
　　　　Makes not amends for his hurt that one time.
¶ Euen so in shippe, the boy that séekes to clime,
By cordes and lines, if either rope doe slippe,
Or hand or foote, as many doe sometime,
Then downe a maine he falles into the shippe.
　　　　Or in the Sea, where hundreth then to one:
　　　　He neuer scapes, ther's one young Sea-man gone.
¶ Yet doe I not forbid to clime at all,
For some must clime, and those I well allow:
But yet I wish the best to feare a fall,
And those that clime at all, to clime, but how?
　　　　When néede requires, and then so carefully,
　　　　As that they come not downe too hastily.
¶ For some must clime, as in assault sometime,
Some men of force must séeke to scale a forte:
Then happy he, that cunningly can clime,
By ropes or Ladders, or by any sorte.
　　　　That is, and he of glory gaines the crowne,
　　　　Thats soonest vp, and latest throwen downe.
¶ So then I say, of climing thus I end,
Who climeth best, findes climing but a toy:
And I would warne each one I count my friend,
For to conceiue in climing little ioy.
　　　　Least that he finde in climing his delight:
　　　　By breake-necke falles to bréede his deadly spight.
¶ And as of climing, so in Fencing now,
Artes much alike, wherein too many ioy:
Which foolish ioy dooth bréede I say to you,
To thousands of your deadly hartes annoy.
　　　　As in my minde, a most accursed sort:
　　　　To bréede delight in such despightfull sport.

Fencing, The eleuenth pleaſure.

Now ſir, this ioy in Arte of great Defence,
    Which of Offence may rather well be namde:
Is not obtaind without ſome great expence,
Nor yet without ſome lim or other lambe.
            Except by hap, you chance to ſcape the worſt,
            And yet you part then with your noddle burſt,
¶ And let me but demaund this queſtion now,
Will you be pleaſd with him that brake your pate?
Or will you not, almoſt you care not how,
Séeke your reuenge, and beare him deadly hate,
            Untill you be reuenged in like ſorte:
            And tell me then, is not this prettie ſporte?
¶ Perhaps againe, you haue your eye thruſt out,
Or catch a ſcratch croſſe ouerthwart your face:
Or elſe be ſwadled roughly round aboute,
Both ſhoulders, ſides, armes, legs, and euery place.
            At parting now, Sir when you féele the ſmart:
            Will you not thinke Fencing a ioyfull Arte?
¶ By Fencing growes our termes of the Brauado,
Our foines and thruſts, the deadly ſtabbe and all:
Which ſome more finely call a Stabbado,
And ſome a blowe, a cleanly wipe can call.
            And ſome a rake, that croſſeth both the ſhinnes,
            Now with ſuch ſtuffe this ioyfull ſport beginnes.
¶ Lie héere, lie there, ſtrike out your blow at length,
 Strike and thruſt with him, looke to your dagger hand:
Beléeue me ſir, you beare a gallant ſtrength,
But chuſe your ground, at vantage where to ſtand,
            And kéepe a loofe for catching too much harme:
            Beware the button of your Buckler arme.
¶ With other termes that were too long to tell,
Beſides, my ſelfe haue ſmall ſkill in that arte,
But this I wot, vnto my coſt too well,
A waſters end hath made my ſhoulders ſmart.
            And when by chaunce I caught a ſmoaking blow,
            I put it vp, or take two or thrée moe.
¶ And ſure I thinke, who doth in déede delight,
To follow Fencing, as ſome ſwaſhers doe:
Shall be thereby ſo boldened for to fight,
As willfull end, in time will bring them to.

Except that God doe giue them grace in déede,
To vſe their arte but in defence at néede.
¶ And vſed ſo, it will not doe amiſſe,
And ſo I thinke ſome ſkill is requiſite:
But I cannot like very well of this,
That any man ſhould ſo therein delight:
　　As he ſhould ſet therein ſo great a ioy,
　　As many doe, vnto their great annoy.
¶ What ſhould I néede, of Fencing more to write,
Well uſed I thinke it is a pretie arte:
But by your leaue, who doth therein delight,
Shall buy his pleaſure, with his bodies ſmart.
　　And ſo I end, vſe it to ſaue your life:
　　But let it not make you to liue in ſtrife.
¶ And then in Gods name, vſe it at your will,
So that you vſe it to your owne defence:
But if in fight, you chance your foe to kill,
His death will ſure abide your conſcience.
　　Yet for all that vſe it but to defend:
　　And learne the arts, it will not much offend.
¶ But as I ſaid before, I ſay againe,
Learne it, but loue it not, in any wiſe:
Leaſt little pleaſure bréede your paine,
By hurt, by maime, or deadly ieopardies.
　　And thinke it but an arte of ſmall delight,
　　Which many wayes doth worke full great deſpight.
¶ But leauing now, of Fencing more to write,
There is as now another kinde of ioy:
Wherein ſome men, doe take ſo great delight,
As that in time it bréedes their great annoy,
　　They toyle themſelues, and thrift they throw away,
　　And lame their legs to learne a fooliſh play.

Tennis, The twelft pleaſure.

What ſport is it to cut a Ball in kinde,
Or ſtrike a Ball into the hazard fine:
Or bandie Balles, to flie againſt the winde,
Or ſtrike a ball low, leuell ore the line.
　　Or make a Chaſe or hazard for a game,
　　Then with a brickle wall to winne the ſame.

¶ Oh braue delightes, but he that thinkes vpon
The vnknowne charge that groweth by the same,
Will say, when once his store of coyne is gone,
Of all sportes, Tennis is a costly game.
    Which cost considered, soone will driue away,
    The deere delight that growes by Tennis play.
¶ Yet will I not dispraise the Tennis so,
That I would wish no man should vse the same.
For by the game no hurt is like to grow,
Except a man doe too much vse the same.
    For I would haue it vsde for exercise:
    In some cold mornings, and not otherwise.
¶ For as I said in other things before,
Tis not the thing, but the delight therein:
That makes or marres, delightes or greeueth sore,
Then take good heede, when first you doe begin.
    To take delight in any kinde of thing:
    For too much ioy doth after sorrow bring.
¶ Then vse the Tennis, wisely now and than,
To exercise your lustlesse limmes withall:
And doe not thinke to doe more then you can,
With labouring and toyling at a ball,
    Least that you thinke, in stead of sweete delight:
    With painefull toyle you buy a deere despight.
¶ And as of Tennis, so againe I finde:
In other sportes, as shooting, bowling too:
Wherein too many, so much set their minde,
As all day long they little els can doe.
    Would they but way the woes thereby they win:
    And they would leaue their fond delight therein.

Shooting, The thirteenth pleasure.

What sporte it is to see an arrow flie,
    A gallant archer cleanly draw his bowe?
In shooting off, againe how cunningly,
He hath his loose, in letting of it goe?
    To nocke it sure, and draws it to the head:
    And then flie out, hold straight, and strike it dead.
¶ With other termes that Archers long haue vsde,
As blow winde, stoupe, ah, downe the winde a bowe:
Tush, sayes another, he may be excusde,

Since the laſt marke, the winde doth greater grow.
      At laſt he claps in the white ſuddainely,
      Then oh well ſhot the ſtanders by doe cry.
¶ And that one ſhoote, is euen enough to make,
Him ſell his coate for ſtore of bowe and ſhafts:
The coſt whereof will make his hart to ake,
And make him draw but few delightfull drafts.
      Therefore ſay I, in ſhooting the delight,
      Dooth likewiſe bréede with pleaſure ſome deſpight.
¶ I doo not ſpeake particularly of all,
The harmes that hap vnto an archers purſe:
As bow may breake, ſtring cracke, and feathers fall,
With other haps, that makes them ſweare and curſe.
      As when ſometime there raines a ſuddaine ſhowre,
      That bowe and ſhafts may marre all in an howre.
¶ Therefore vſe ſhooting as an exerciſe,
To paſſe the time, but loue it not too much:
Leaſt with the ſport you finde the coſtly price,
Doe make your hart ſuch deare delights to grutch.
      Therefore vſe it, but as a pretie toy:
      To paſſe the day, but count it not a ioy.

Bowling, The fourtéenth pleaſure.

And now to Bowles, a pretty kinde of ſport.
  Wherein ſo many take ſo great delight:
That euery day ſuch numbers doe reſort.
To bowling Allies, that both day and night,
      If light would ſerue they would not be away,
      But waſt their wealth vpon that fooliſh play.
¶ How ſome delight, to ſée a round Bowle run,
Smoothely away, vntill he catch a rub:
Then hold thy bias, if that caſt were wun,
The game were vp as ſure then as a club.
      Then vpright Bowles, that néede not any banke,
      And for a game, a fine throw in the cranke.
¶ But if they markt their money run away,
Their coyne to croſſe quite byas from their purſe:
T'would make them leaue that coſtly kinde of play,
And liking take in bowling ſporte the wurſe.
      And yet the ſport well vſde, will yéeld delight:

But loue it not, for then it bréedes despight.
¶ For ioy in games to other kinde of ioyes,
Wherein some men, their chiefe delight repose:
Which wayed well, may well be thought but toyes,
Wherein both cost and labour eke we lose.

    As Fishing, Fowling, and such like delights:
    Which some doe loue to follow dayes and nights.
¶ But loe, beholde, what great delight we finde,
In Fishing first, in diuers sundry sortes:
With Nets, and Angles, Wéeles, and other kinde,
Or pretie ginnes, which yéelde delightfull sportes.

    And with the sportes, lets sée the spight withall:
    That oftentimes in Fishing dooth befall.

Fishing, The fiftéene pleasure.

Some take delight with Angle for to stand,
Néere halfe a day, to catch a Pickerell:
And standing so with Angle in his hand,
Perhaps he takes a paltry Shotrell.

    That what a man hath taken with such paine,
    He straight would throwe into the brooke againe.
¶ Some with a worme doe angle for an éele,
Some for a Carpe doe angle with a Snaile:
But if the hooke doe catch within a Wéele,
Then must of force the fishers cunning faile.

    For loose the hooke, and fray thy fish away,
    And stand againe without a bite all day.
¶ And is it not a wearie kinde of sport,
To angle all day for a foolish dish:
And loose the hooke in such despightfull sorte,
And that perhaps or ere you catch a fish.

    Me thinkes it should be such a foule despight,
    As I should take in angling no delight.
¶ Some for a Troute, will angle with a flie,
Some for a Roche, a gentill make their baite:
Some make their Flies of colours cunningly,
Of silke and haire, a prettie fine deceite

    For foolish fishe, and yet tis but a toy,
    Unworthie farre for to be thought a ioy.

¶ And yet some men doe so herein delight,
As in the making of these foolish flies,
They will attend their worke both day and night,
And in the morning vp betimes arise.

     And to the brooke, and angle there all day,
     And yet perhaps come emptie hand away.

¶ Then iudge what spight the Fisher doth abide,
To loose his paines, and yet receiue no sport:
If I said naught, yet some that well haue tride,
The like themselues, and fished in like sorte,

     Will say with me, it is a spightfull toy,
     Which with much griefe doth yéeld but little ioy.

¶ Some loue to fish with trammell, drags, bow nets,
With casting nets, and nets of other sortes:
Wherein some man his pleasure wholy sets,
And greatly cares not for no other sportes.

     But let him looke hée doe not play the foole,
     That with his Net, he fling into the poole.

¶ And he that dreggeth like a water dog,
And wades to knées to catch a dish of fish:
And in the end doth draw vp but a frog,
Is not he well at ease with such a dish?

     Who would not be a Fisherman to gaine,
     Such daintie morsels to requite his paine?

¶ Perhaps againe, with wading well all day,
He catch such cold as sicknes doe insue:
An Ague then will make him shaking say,
Too late (alas) my fond delight I rue.

     This wading sport, dooth yéelde so great annoy,
     As that I finde in Fishing little ioy.

¶ Now some againe, besides their labour lost,
And falling sicke with catching colde by wet:
By mashes breake, may hap to be at cost,
For Lines, and Corkes, and mending of the Net,

     And that dayes worke, the mending be so déere,
     As fishing scarce will pay for in a yéere.

¶ What should I say of Fishing more then this,
Fishing vsde well, may séeme a prettie sporte:
But no delight but may be vsde amisse,
Then take delight in fishing in such sorte:

     As that it proue not too much to your cost:
     Nor yet lament your labour too much lost.

¶ For Fiſhing ſport I can not iuſtly blame,
If it be vſed as it ought to be:
But ſuch delight as ſome haue in the ſame,
I cannot chuſe but blame, when as I ſée
      Some ſicke, ſome drownd, with following the ioy,
      They doe conceiue in ſuch a fooliſh toy.
¶ And as of fiſhing, ſo againe I finde,
In Fowling to the ioy that ſome conceiue:
Would ſome that Fowle, but wiſely way in minde,
And they ſhould ſoone their ouer-ſights perceiue.
      When they eſtéeme thoſe thinges delightfull ioyes,
      Which as they vſe, doe proue deſpightfull toyes.

Fowling, The ſixtéenth pleaſure.

Some men will toyle in water, froſt and ſnow,
To ſet a Lymetwig for a fooliſh Snite:
And glad for colde, his fingers ends to blow,
And ſo ſtand plodding all day long till night.
      And for wild Fowle, euen like a peaking mome,
      To catch a Snipe, and beare a tame foole home.
¶ Now ſome againe, goe ſtalking with a Gun,
To kill a Herne, a Shooluerd or a Crane:
Who plodding ſo, ere fowling time be done,
Doe miſſe the Fowle, and bréede their ſuddaine bane.
      As if the péece ſhould breake in cracks or flawes,
      Or elſe recoyle, and ſtrike a two his iawes.
¶ Or elſe the winde may hap to blowe the fire,
Upon his face, and marre his viſage quite:
Then tell me now, what he would not deſire,
To goe a Fowling for ſuch ſwéete delight.
      Tuſh, many moe ſuch miſchiefes doe I know,
      Which Fowlers finde, but were two long to ſhow.
¶ But leaſt that ſome ſhould count me for a foole,
For to diſpraiſe the ſport in Fowling quite:
I ſay no more, but fall not in the poole,
Catch not a Snipe, in ſetting for a Snite.
      Looke to the Péece, kéepe thy face from the fire,
      And Fowle in Gods name to thine owne deſire.
¶ But loue it not too much, but as it is,

Eſtéeme it ſo, a hard cold ſport in déede,
Which vſde aright, is pleaſant, but amiſſe,
Yéeldes diuers griefes, therefore no more the néede.
        Follow the ſport, nor take therein delight:
        Too much I meane, leaſt it doe worke thée ſpight.
¶ And thus I leaue to ſpeake more of ſuch ſportes,
As with delight doe bréede as great deſpight,
And of delights in other ſundry ſortes,
That dayly grow, I meane my minde to write.
        Which waied well, are all but fooliſh toyes:
        Which with great griefes doe yéeld but little ioyes.

Studies, The ſeuentéene pleaſure.

Some men delight all day to breake their braine,
With ſtudie ſtrange, as ſome will ſpend their time:
In Phiſicke, Lawe, and ſome will take great paine,
In Muſickes arte, and ſome will ſéeke to clime,
        The ſkies by ſtudie in Aſtronomie:
        Some compaſſe countries by Coſmography.
¶ Some men great paines in Nigromancie take,
Some loue to ſtudie Phiſiognomie:
Which ſtudies make both braines and hart to ake,
And maketh many ſtarke mad ere they dye.
        Some loue to be thought good Palmeſters,
        And thouſands ſéeke to be Philoſophers.
¶ Some loue to ſtudie moſt Arithmatike,
In Logicke ſome doe dayly beate their braine:
And ſome delight as much in Rethoricke,
And ſome doe ioy in hiſtories againe.
        But very few doe take delight in déede,
        To ſtudie that whereof they moſt haue néed.
¶ By which who loues, ſhall finde a heauenly ioy,
A ioy beſides that neuer will decay:
And with the ioy, yéeldes no iote of annoy,
But teacheth vs to heauen the ready way.
        Which ſtudie is Diuinitie by name:
        God graunt vs all to ſtudie well the ſame.

Phiſicke, The eightéene pleaſure.

In Phiſickes arte, lets ſée what ioy we finde,
We heale the ſicke by Medicines we make:
By vertues rare, of hearbes of ſundry kinde,
By waters, oyles, and how we ought to take,
  Each in his kinde, how beſt it may preuaile:
  This Phiſickes arte doth ſhew for our auaile.

¶ But if the man that is of greateſt ſkill,
Haue not great care, in vſing of this arte:
May miniſter a medicine to kill,
When as he thinkes, to eaſe the ſicke mans ſmart.
  And who doth ſo may thinke himſelfe accurſt,
  And Phiſicke count of ſtudies all the worſt.

¶ But he that takes ſuch care in each reſpect,
And feares the worſt, and ſéekes to doe his beſt,
Regardes the cauſe, doth not the time neglect,
But wiſely workes to bréede his patients reſt.
  In Phiſickes arte, well hath he taken paine:
  Gods fauour, and good Fame, ſhall be his gaine.

¶ But if he ſo be ſetled in that arte,
And that he count that ſtudie for his ioy:
How beſt to ſéeke to eaſe the bodies ſmart,
And ſéeke no medicine for the ſoules annoy.
  When that himſelfe in fine, of force muſt die?
  Oh then where ſhall his ſoule for comfort cry?

¶ Let him haue ſpent ſome time in ſacred writ,
And in that ſtudie ſet his chiefe delight,
And he ſhall there ſoone finde a medicine fit,
To ſalue and ſaue his ſoule from perrill quite.
  Oh bleſſed ſtudie, that doth ſhew reliefe,
  To ſoule and bodie in their greateſt griefe.

¶ In holy writ we learne how to lament,
Our ſinfull life, wherewith we God offend:
There we are taught our ſinnes for to repent,
And there we learne how ſoone we may amend.
  There doe we reade, that God muſt be the meane,
  To cleanſe our ſoules from all offences cleane.

¶ There doe we finde, that penitence procures,
Pardon of God, with pardon, pittie to:
Which pittie ſends ſuch comfort, as ſoone cures

The greateſt hurt that worldly woes can doe.
  And there we finde, Gods mercie yéelds at laſt,
  The ioyes of heauen, when worldly woes are paſt.
¶ If Phiſicke then may yéeld ſo great delight,
For teaching vs to ſaue the bodies ſmart:
The ſtudie then that ſoule and bodie quite,
Ridds of all woe, doth it not paſſe all arte,
  Yes out of doubt, that yéeldes the onely ioyes:
  To which comparde, all ſtudies are but toyes.
¶ Then ſtudie Phiſicke for neceſſitie,
To heale a hurt, or eaſe the ſicke-mans ſmart:
But let thy ioy be in Diuinitie,
Which waied well, excelleth euery arte.
  For Phiſicke ſerues but for the bodies griefe,
  Diuinitie doth yéelde the ſoules reliefe.

Lawe, The ninetéene pleaſure.

And leauing thus of Phiſicke more to write,
 Lets ſée what ioy in ſtudie of the Lawe,
Some men thereby perhaps doe take delight,
To make wrong right, and right not worth a ſtraw.
  Which yéelds God knowes, the poore mans great deſpight
  To be by wrong bereaued of his right.
¶ And when perhaps the Lawier calls to minde,
The wrong ſo wrought, and weighes the poore mans caſe,
He doth in time within his conſcience finde,
Such great vnreſt, as reſteth in no place.
  And thinke you then by Law what gréeuous ioy,
  Which bréedeth ſo the ſecrete hartes annoy.
¶ Yet will I not ſo much diſpraiſe the Law,
That I would wiſh no man to like the ſame:
For then I might be counted well a Daw,
But this I ſay, who ſéekes himſelfe to frame,
  To ſtudie Law, I wiſh him firſt of all,
  To ſtudie of Diuinitie to fall.
¶ There firſt to learne his ſtudie how to vſe,
To learne the Law, thereby his owne to kéepe:
And not as ſome the ſtudie doe abuſe.
By ſhifts in Law, in others rights to créepe.
  And ſo by wrong to purchaſe worldly wealth,

As that it proue a hurt to his soules health.
¶ Then first peruse the sacred Lawes of God,
How he doth will, that we our Lawes should vse,
And iustly how he scourgeth with his rod,
All such as scorne, or else his Lawes refuse.
　　And then to Law, to learne to kéepe thy right:
　　And helpe thy friend, let be thy whole delight.
¶ But in respect of holy Lawes I say,
Account our studies in the Lawes but toyes:
When scripture showes the onely ready way,
For to attaine to euerlasting ioyes.
　　Let then I say, Deuinitie be thought,
　　The onely ioy, to which the best is nought.

Astronomie and Phisiognomie. The twentie Pleasure.

So could I write to of Astronomie,
　By which we clime into the loftie skie:
And so againe of Phisiognomie,
Whereby by face, we wonders doe descrie,
　　Diuinitie heaues vs aboue the skie,
　　And doth to vs the power of God descrie.

Cosmographie, and Philosophie, The
one and twentie Pleasure.

Now sée the ioy got by Cosmographie,
　We compasse countries, learnedly by arte:
And what delight by fine Philosophie,
By reason strange, to proue on eyther parte,
　　False iudgement true, and further to descrie:
　　Secretes in nature, by Philosophie.
¶ By wholy writ, the way to heauen we finde,
A countrie farre aboue the loftie skie:
By sacred Lawes, we can confute in kinde,
The vniust cause, and proue the contrary.
　　By Scriptures eke, Gods nature plaine we finde:
　　Iust, mercifull, and to his seruants kinde.
¶ Now sée how farre this studie doth surpasse,
All studies else, what so without respect:

Then may he be iuſtly thought an aſſe,
Which dooth this ſtudie any thing neglect?
  And counteth not all other ſtudies toyes,
  Comparde to this, which yéeldeth heauenly ioyes.

Muſicke, The [two and] twentie pleaſure.

In Muſicke now, a great delight we finde,
 And ſure it is a prettie kinde of arte:
But oh that we would ſettle once our minde,
To tune our tongues, with ſound of humble hart.
  To ſing due lawde vnto the Lorde on hie:
  Oh that would ſéeme an heauenly harmonie.
¶ And now the ioyes got by Arithmaticke,
To number much within a little time:
And ſome doe loue to rowle in Rethoricke,
Some beſt like proſe, and ſome delight in Rime.
  And yet all theſe conſidered well in minde,
  But trifling toyes the true Diuine doth finde.

Diuinitie, The twentie thrée pleaſure.

Diuinitie dooth number out our dayes,
 And ſhowes our life, ſtill fading as a flowre:
Bids vs beware of wanton wicked wayes,
For we are ſure to liue no certaine howre.
  Arithmaticke doth number worldly toyes,
  Diuinitie innumerable ioyes.
¶ Then iudge I pray which yéeldes the more delight,
Diuinitie, then chuſe it for thy ioy:
Studie that chiefe, and labour day and night,
By that to learne to ſhield thée from annoy.
  And thou ſhalt finde it ſalueth euery ſore:
  And ſaues the ſoule, and what ioy can be more?
¶ By Rethoricke, now ſome doe take delight,
To paint a fable with a gallant gloſe:
But no ſuch tale is gratefull in Gods ſight,
Beſides, he will each ſecrete ſhift diſcloſe.
  His tale is beſt before the Lorde, who ſayes,
  He doth in hart repent his ſinfull dayes.

¶ Who dooth in déed his sinfull life confesse,
Who pardon craues, and calles to God for grace,
His tale is heard, him God doth rightly blesse,
And eke in heauen prouides for him a place.

     God graunt vs all our prayers so to vse:
     That he may not our penitence refuse.

¶ Now some againe delight in Histories,
To reade the Acts of some couragious Knight:
To thinke vpon the gallant victories,
To reade againe the order of the fight.

     And doe such stories bréede delight in déede?
     Then take delight the Scriptures for to reade.

¶ There shalt thou finde how Christ a battell fought,
Against the deuill and his cursed traine:
Subdude them all, their force preuailed nought,
But all were driuen into eternall paine.

     Blessed be he that so hath brought in thrall,
     Him that would else haue surely slaine vs all.

¶ And tell me then, although some valiant Knight,
Did conquere Realmes, and by his force of armes
Subdued Princes by his onely might,
And made them know his force vnto their harmes,

     Yet thinke of him, that by his onely might,
     Did saue both thée, and all the world by fight.

¶ Oh valiant acte, and worthie to be read,
Who sau'd our liues, who else had sure bene slaine,
And further when our bodies here be dead,
Hath sau'd our soules from euerlasting paine.

     God graunt vs all vnder that Christ to fight,
     Who so our soules hath saued by his might.

¶ And of good déedes, to reade doost thou delight?
That worthie are for to be borne in minde,
Then reade how Christ vnto the blinde gaue sight,
Healed the sicke in body and in minde,

     Did giue the lame their limmes, and what else more?
     Gaue the diseasde a salue for euery sore.

¶ Where can you reade, of one so good a man,
Tushe, there is none without exception:
Let vs delight our selues there now and than,
His great good déedes to reade and looke vpon.

     And we shall finde thereby such heauenly ioyes:
     As we shall count all Stories else but toyes.

¶ For if we doe to minde, his goodneſſe call,
How great a good he hath beſtowed on vs:
By his deare death and bloud to ſaue vs all,
Are we not bound to thinke onely Ieſus,
      To be in déede the Author of our ioy,
      And onely he that kéepes vs from annoy?
¶ Yes out of doubt, and therefore thus I end,
God graunt vs all, to take him for our ioy:
To loue our God, which is our onely friend,
That ſaues our ſoules, and bodies from annoy.
      And to eſtéeme all worldly thinges but toyes:
      And ſet in Chriſt our all and onely ioyes.

FINIS.

SELECTED SHAKESPEARE APOCRYPHA

- http://en.wikipedia.org/wiki/Shakespeare_Apocrypha contains links to texts of many of the Shakespeare apocrypha.
- "To the Queen, by the Players" https://en.wikipedia.org/wiki/To_the_Queen, which Jonathan Bate has proposed as by Shakespeare. A nice poem in any case.
- "The Funeral Elegy" http://shakespeareauthorship.com/elegy.html now attributed to John Ford
- "Shall I die?" https://en.wikisource.org/wiki/Shall_I_die%3F now attributed to John Ford

FURTHER READING

There is a great deal written on the Shakespeare authorship controversy. Most of it is political and highly biased, one way or another. Here are a couple of the more interesting.

Anyone seriously interested in the study of Shakespeare's authorship should read Mark Anderson's *Shakespeare by Another Name*, now available in eBook format with a new introduction. Anderson's book concentrates, refreshingly, on simple evidence. Anderson, a science writer, knows what a fact is and has put together a level-headed and highly readable summary of the Oxfordian case.

James Shapiro's *Contested Will* has perceptive things to say about the psychology of Shakespearean fandom, but his facts can be unreliable. As an example, he should know that many plays described as "new" were what we would call "revised"— *Henry VIII* was almost certainly not newly written in 1613.

Kevin Gilvary's *Dating Shakespeare's Plays* summarizes the modern evidence for the dating of Shakespeare's work.

Richard Roe's *A Shakespeare Guide to Italy* gathers the evidence of Shakespeare's knowledge of Italy.

For additional useful sources, see the footnotes to my novel *Chasing Shakespeares*, available on www.sarahsmith.com.

And if you are in the mood for a larger collection of speculations, I would be delighted if you choose to read *Chasing Shakespeares*.

ENDNOTES

For ease of reading, you can also find these notes at my Web site, www.sarahsmith.com.

[1] There is an online version at
http://www.gutenberg.org/ebooks/1547 .
See a picture of the More MS at
http://en.wikipedia.org/wiki/File:Sir_Thomas_More_Hand_D.jpg

[2] Pollard, Alfred W., W.W. Greg, Edward Maunde Thompson, John Dover Wilson, and R.W. Chambers, *Shakespeare's Hand in the Play of Sir Thomas More.* Cambridge, Cambridge University Press, 1923.

[3] Atria Books, 2003; Washington Square Books, 2004; Max Light Books, 2022, with new material. Also available as an eBook.

[4] Rice [i.e. Rhys] Jones. *Item* Lycenced unto him a booke intitled *the payne of pleasur[e]* compiled by N. BRITTEN. Transcribed in Edward Arber, *Transcript of the Registers of the Stationers' Company of London* 2:152. London: Privately printed, 1 October 1875. Celeste Turner points out that Jones had a reputation for foisting publications on Breton; see her *Anthony Munday, An Elizabethan Man of Letters.* Berkeley CA: University of California Press, 1928, p. 9. This *SR* entry may argue that the poem was written as early as 1578; conservatively, though, it cannot be dated earlier than 1580, and that is the assumption I have used here. Jones had previously printed Breton's *A Flourish upon Fancy*.

[5] Munday's works ca 1580 were printed by one of three printers, Charlewood, John Allde, or Henry Denham. At this period John Charlewood was in possession of an unusual black-letter typeface, in which double O was an infinity-shaped ligature and double E was always printed with an acute accent over the first E. Both are visible in the line here:

𝕴𝖓 𝖋𝖚𝖗𝖙𝖍𝖊𝖗 𝖞𝖊́𝖗𝖊𝖘, 𝖜𝖊 𝖜𝖆𝖓𝖉𝖊𝖗 𝖙𝖔 𝖆𝖓𝖉 𝖋𝖗𝖔,

Other books Charlewood printed around 1580 also show the ée, e.g. "T.T."'s (Thomas Twyne's?) *A View of Certain Wonderful Effects* (1578), Munday's *A Courtly Controversy between Love and Learning* (1581), and Munday's *Watch-Woord to England* (1584). Charlewood is known to have printed other books for Henry Carr during this period, so the attribution of this book to him seems reasonable.

This typeface had a long, distinguished career. From about 1588 it formed part of the stock of Jacqueline Vautrollier's and Richard Field's shop, and the remnants of it were used as an "antique" font in both editions of *The Treasurie of Auncient and Moderne Times...*, ascribed to Thomas Milles. The first edition of 1613 [STC 17936] is reproduced in EEBO; the second edition, published 1619 and retitled, *Archaio-Ploutos,* is in the collection of the Countway Library, Harvard. By coincidence, as Roger Stritmatter has noted, *Archaio-Ploutos* is dedicated to the Earl of Montgomery—one of the "incomparable Brethren" of the First Folio—and his wife, who was Oxford's youngest daughter.

[6] My thanks to the British Library, and to Anastasia Cox, then of Random House UK, for providing me with Xeroxed copies of both of these. I am grateful also to Widener and Houghton Libraries and to the Countway Library of Medicine, Harvard University.

[7] Steven May, *ibid.*

[8] "Shooting," in "The Paine of Pleasure." *The Paine of Pleasure. Profitable to be perused of the wise, and necessary to be followed by the wanton. Reade with regard.* Honos alit Artes. Imprinted at London for Henrie Car, and are to be solde at his shop in Paules Churchyarde, next to the signe of the holy Lambe. 17. October. 1580. Hereafter referred to in parentheses in the text. The copy I have used is the one in the BL, augmented by the unique title page at Cambridge.

[9] Though 1580 is rather early for a Breton work of this kind; Harvard may base this attribution on the *SR* entry.

[10] [Nicholas Breton] *The vvoorkes of a young wyt, trust up with a Fardell of pretie fancies, profitable to young Poetes, prejudicial to no man, and pleasaunt to every man to pass away idle tyme withall.* Done by N.B. London: Thomas Dawson and Thomas Gardyner, [1577], fol. 7.

[11] *Ibid.*

[12] The *DNB* entry on Munday does not feel his name on the dedications is clear proof of his authorship; the author questions Munday's authorship of "The Paine of Pleasure" in spite of having

seen the complete Pepysian Library copy. *DNB*, "Anthony Munday." The *SR* entry of 1578 also may indicate that the book was a compilation—if the *SR* entry refers to the book we have.

[13] From "Nebuchadnezzar," text taken from the Literature Online version of the *Mutabilitie* poems; henceforth referred to in parentheses in the text as *Mut*. The *Mutabilitie* poems and "Paine" share one rather unusual characteristic, a fondness for extremely heavy punctuation, particularly colons at the ends of lines. However, this is a characteristic shared with other forms of literature meant to be read aloud, such as sermons, and any argument from punctuation in Elizabethan times is a slim reed.

[14] Hertford was a very small castle, and Elizabeth seldom visited there after she became Queen; these obscure lines may suggest someone who knew the Court in its early days, soon after Elizabeth's accession in 1558.

[15] William Kittle, in his *George Gascoigne April 1562 to January 1, 1578, or Edward de Vere, Seventeenth Earl of Oxford 1550-1604*, believes that this must be New Year's Day 1577/8, and concludes that "The Grief of Joy", among other poems, must be Oxford's work. But Kittle fails to take into account the clear similarities between "The Grief of Joy" and other work known to be Gascoigne's, and his work is marred throughout by a desire to "prove" that all of Gascoigne's poetry was written by Oxford (!).

[16] E.g. in Gascoigne, George. *Complete Poems of George Gascoigne*. 2v. Ed. William Carew Hazlitt. [London:] The Roxburghe Library, 1868-70. II, 294, 301. But this is probably a commonplace; as we have seen, Breton also uses it.

[17] Gascoigne, *Works*, II, 265-267. "Meal" comes from the same stem as "cornmeal", "oatmeal": the hours are ground into minutes.

[18] For his edition of 1910, Cunliffe could find only two manuscripts, one of which, Royal MS.18.A.lxi, was Gascoigne's presentation copy to Elizabeth.

[19] Or, if the *SR* entry represents a finished poem, September 1578.

[20] And in any case it is unlike his other work of the period; Gorges wrote almost exclusively love lyrics. See *The Poems of Sir Arthur Gorges*, ed. Helen Estabrook Sandeson. Oxford: Clarendon, 1953.

[21] Arundel is also a dedicated practitioner of rocker verse; see Steven W. May, *The Elizabethan Courtier Poets: The Poems and their Contexts* (Columbia MO and London: University of Missouri Press, 1991), pp. 352-353.

[22] Lord Burghley's extant poetry is also very unlike this poem.

[23] May, *Elizabethan Courtier Poets*, p. 368.

[24] Given his interest in training horses, he may have appeared in the tiltyard, as many courtier poets did, including the Earl of Cumberland, Fulke Greville, Sir Christopher Hatton, the Earl of Arundel, Sir Henry Lee, and Henry Neel.

[25] Raphael Holinshed, *The First and Second Volumes of Chronicles*, London 1587, quoted in Heidi Brayman Hackel, "The 'Great Variety' of Readers." in *A Companion to Shakespeare*, ed. David Scott Kastan (London and Malden MA: Blackwell Publishers, 1999), p. 148.

[26] I leave aside the question of who wrote the poems in Gascoigne's *An Hundred Sundrie Flowers of English Poesy*.

[27] One of the portions of "The Grief of Joy" that emphatically does not appear in "The Paine of Pleasure" is the praise of Oxford's wife.

[28] It is perhaps significant, but probably not, that the British Library copy of *The Paine of Pleasure* is bound together with a copy of *The Paradise of Dainty Devices*.

[29] As noted above, he was also the stepfather of Nicholas Breton. See C.T. Prouty, *George Gascoigne, Elizabethan Courtier, Soldier, and Poet.* New York: Columbia University Press, 1942.

[30] Gascoigne also mentions Oxford in one of his poems, and "The Grief of Joy" mentions both Oxford's sister Mary and his estranged wife among the beauties of the court. Gascoigne's *Supposes*, performed at Gray's Inn in 1566, is considered to be a source for *The Taming of the Shrew*.

[31] His youngest daughter's husband and her husband's brother are the "Glorious Brethren," the dedicatees of the First Folio.

[32] See also Roger Stritmatter, *The Marginalia of Edward de Vere's Geneva Bible: Providential Discovery, Literary Reasoning, and Historical Consequence.* Northampton MA: The Oxenford Press, 2001.

[33] He would also have had access to Sir Thomas Smith's extensive library, the large library of Gray's Inn, and probably to the library of his friend and fellow-ward, the Earl of Rutland. He might have had access to Elizabeth's library.

[34] He may also have composed music, e.g. "The Earl of Oxford's March."

[35] Verily Anderson, *The De Veres of Castle Hedingham.* Lavenham, Suffolk: Terence Dalton Ltd., 1993, p. 122.

[36] Celeste Turner speculates on the dates of Munday's

acquaintance with Oxford and trip to Italy in *Anthony Munday* and decides that Munday was in Rome from fall 1578-July 1579; but her facts can be unreliable.

[37] *DNB,* "Anthony Munday."

[38] Since "The Paine of Pleasure" formed the principal part of a volume from which Munday would have got some financial gain, it may have been an act of generosity as well as trust. If so, it would fit in with Oxford's other generous acts toward literary men, such as his writing a dedicatory preface to Thomas Bedingfield's *Cardanus Comfort* (1573).

[39] Steven May, "The Earl of Oxford's Poetry in Context."

[40] Data from Steven May, *ibid.* In conversation with me, Steven May noted that Oxford may have written didactic poetry; we know only that none of his identified surviving poetry is didactic.

[41] "His mind not quietly settled, he writeth this," from *The Paradise of Dainty Devices,* 1576; in *Letters and Poems of Edward, Earl of Oxford,* ed. Katherine Chiljan (n.p.: n.p., 1998), p. 168.

[42] "The complaint of a lover, wearing black and tawny," *ibid.,* p. 164.

[43] *Ibid.*

[44] Michael D. Bristol, "Shakespeare the Myth." In *A Companion to Shakespeare,* ed. Kastan, p. 489-490.

[45] The Elizabethan term was usually used, derogatorily, of musicians for hire; Shakespeare uses it as a general term of dislike. *OED* s.v. "fiddler".

[46] Shakespeare is supposed to have learned this language from books, but Father John Gerard remarks that it is not easy to use the terms correctly without knowing the sport. He tried to teach them to Robert Southwell: "...I spoke about hunting and falconry, a thing no one could do in correct technical language unless he was familiar with the sport. It is an easy thing to trip up in one's terms, as Father Southwell used to complain...he could not remember and use [the technical terms] when need arose." (*Autobiography of a Hunted Priest,* written 1609, translated by Philip Caraman; Garden City NY: Image Books, 1955, pp. 41-42)

[47] Perhaps Elizabethan slang for "down, boy," addressed to the arrow. Not recorded in *OED* in any sense related to archery.

[48] First recorded use in English of this term in this sense (see *OED* "bravado", definition 1b).

[49] Typo/missing text here? Or is finely "fi-ne-ly"?

[50] Not recorded in *OED.* May be sixteenth-century Italian, or may

be a joke on fencers who use cod-Italian.

[51] The *OED* finds this obscure word used previously only in Gascoigne's *Supposes*, 1566—one of Shakespeare's likely sources for *The Taming of the Shrew*.

[52] The *OED* finds this word used previously only in Anglo-Saxon and in Scottish prose and poetry; this is its first appearance in modern English. The *OED* does not cite any appearances of this word outside works produced in Scotland and Lancashire. E.A. Honigmann suggests that William Shakespeare of Stratford worked for the Hoghton family in Lancashire, from which some of his Scottish/Northron coinages may come. Oxford did military service in Scotland.

[53] First *OED* cited use is 1578, in Lyte's *Dodoes.*

[54] Used both to mean a woodcock and in its modern sense of snipe-hunt or "hunting fools with a mirror":

> And for wild Fowle, euen like a peaking mome,
> To catch a Snipe, and beare a tame foole home.

Compare

> For I mine owne gain'd knowledge should prophane,
> If I would time expend with such [a] Snipe
> (*Othello*, I, iii)

[55] The *OED* knows that there is a distinction, but not what it is; *OED* "snite" n1.

[56] *OED* cites first use 1586, so this is first known use.

[57] Shakespeare is the second cited user of this word; see *OED* "bias", definition 2.a.

[58] *OED* cites first use 1572.

[59] First *OED* use in the sense of "keep score" is not until the nineteenth century, but the author may be using it here in that sense, as a pun. The figurative senses of *cross* and *bias* in the next line support that reading.

[60] Compare Shakespeare's use of similar terminology, above.

[61] Earlier than any cited *OED* use; see *OED* "semibreve". See also *OED* "fain."

[62] *OED* "bricole".

[63] *OED* "brickwall".

[64] Compare Shakespeare's use of tennis terms. He refers casually to tennis or uses tennis metaphors in six plays: *Pericles, King Henry VIII, Much Ado about Nothing, Hamlet, Henry IV part 2,* and *Henry V*:

> When we have match'd our rackets to these balls,

> We will in France, by God's grace, play a set
> Shall strike his father's crown into the hazard.
> Tell him he hath made a match with such a wrangler
> That all the courts of France will be disturb'd
> With chaces....

[65] In *OED*. Robert Greene is the first cited person to use "caper" as a term in dancing, in 1592; Shakespeare is the second.

[66] Before first cited use in *OED*. Robert Greene is the first citation, 1592.

[67] Before first cited use in *OED*.

[68] Repeated (see below), but a typo?

[69] In the original:

> In further years, we fall in miserie,
> From virtues line, and light in sinful snare.
> In further years, we wander too and fro,
> And last in age, God knoweth howe we die.

[70] In the original: do

[71] Indulgent

[72] In the original: herself

[73] *OED* "modest" 2: "Having a moderate or humble estimate of one's own abilities or merits; disinclined to bring oneself into notice; becomingly diffident or unassuming; unobtrusive, retiring, bashful; not bold or forward."

[74] In the original: work.

[75] For the next several stanzas, the author experiments with rhyming between stanzas as well as within them.

[76] In the original: to

[77] *OED* 2: "Rusted, corroded, tarnished," as well as "evil." Cf. *2 Henry IV*, IV.iv. 72: "The canker'd heaps of strange-achievéd gold."

[78] *OED* 7b: "Forge," with a pun on some of its other meanings.

[79] In the original: vaur

[80] In the original: sholue

[81] In the original: Goes

[82] *OED* first cites 1600 in Nicholas Breton's *Pasquin's Fools-Cap*. Cf. "mad-headed" in *1 Henry IV*, II.

[83] In the original: a do

[84] *sic*. Hight?

[85] This and the previous two lines are garbled?

[86] In the original: And dispossesse him of his honour quite.

[87] *OED* "shoe" 2.e.

[88] In the original: stands upon no ground

[89] *OED* 1.b: "A puncture or wound in the quick or sole of the foot of a horse." A technical term in farriery. First *OED* citation 1607.

[90] The vertical distance from which the hawk stoops to its kill.

[91] A large short-winged hawk, used in wooded areas.

[92] "Decide to wander," gad about.

[93] To "seel" a hawk's eyes is to sew them shut for training purposes or for transport (*OED* "seel" v.2). This does not seem to be the meaning aimed for. Possibly the author means "seal" or "sile", which mean "confined" or "marked" or even "[made to] faint or fall down" (*OED* "seal", "sile") or "taken the happy or opportune moment" (*OED* "sele")? But this is mysterious.

[94] Tercel.

[95] The female (lanner) and male (lanneret) of the Mediterranean species *F. lanarius* or *F. feldeggi (OED).*

[96] In the original: throughly

[97] A nice set of bawdy puns.

[98] In the original: Breves and Semibreves

[99] *OED* "fain" v.1: "To take delight in."

[100] A possible topical allusion here; unidentified.

[101] In the original: makes

[102] *OED* "ungracious" 2: "unfortunate, unlucky, unfavorable"; cf. 3.b. and 4, "low- mannered", countrified, or rude.

[103] crue; French crue, crowd? OED "crew" 3.a.: "A number of persons gathered together in association; a company." Cf. the modern "krewe."

[104] *OED* "shrew" 1.a: "a wicked, evil-disposed, or malignant man; a mischievous or vexatious person; a rascal, villain."

[105] *OED* "clap" n.1, 6: "A stroke, blow, or shock of misfortune."

[106] Unrecorded variant of "caper"? See footnote 66.

[107] *OED* "cross-point".

[108] *OED* "chin-bone": if in the meaning of chin, obsolete by this period.

[109] *OED* "daw": n. 2.: "A silly fellow, a simpleton or fool."

[110] A much richer word then than now, meaning "beautifully," "without help," or "altogether, quite, entirely." Shakespeare uses the latter in *Hamlet,* I.i.137. "Enough, by itself, to make him climb," with perhaps a pun on the other senses of the word.

[111] ="Scions"? *OED* "ungracious" 2: "unfortunate, unlucky, unfavorable"; cf. 3.b. and 4, "low-mannered", countrified, or rude. The sense seems to be, "Now, again, some unlucky/low-mannered scions/youths," with a pun on the gardening meaning of "graft," "graft themselves to three trees at once," i.e. to the gallows.

[112] *OED* "willingly" 1.a.: "deliberately, willfully, intentionally." So used by Shakespeare.

[113] Probably a proverbial phrase, which I have not traced.

[114] *OED* "overthwart" 1: "Over from side to side, so as to cross something; across, athwart; crosswise, transversely." Also

[115] *OED* "swaddle" 3: "To beat soundly." Colloquial usage first used ca. 1570.

[116] *OED* "bravado" n 1: "Boastful or threatening behavior; ostentatious display of courage or boldness; bold or daring action intended to intimidate or to express defiance; often, an assumption of courage or hardihood to conceal felt timidity, or to carry one out of a doubtful or difficult position." The first recorded uses of the term postdate this poem.

[117] *OED* "foin" n2: "A thrust or push with a pointed weapon," such as a fencing épée. Shakespeare also uses "foin" in a sexual sense.

[118] Not recorded in *OED*. May be a joke; see note 50.

[119] *OED* "wipe" 2.a.: "A slashing blow, a sweeping cut, a swipe."

[120] *OED* "rake" n3 2.b.: "A pass in fencing."

[121] Thus in the text, *a loofe*. Either "aloof" or "a loose", i.e. hold your sword loosely. A sword held tightly is more easily knocked or spun out of the fencer's hand.

[122] *OED* "waster" n2 1: "A wooden sword or a foil used in sword-exercise and fencing."

[123] A blow hard enough to make the clothes "smoke" with dust; cf. *OED* "smoke" v. 4: "To smart, to suffer severely."

[124] *OED* "swasher" n2: a swashbuckler. The first recorded citation is from 1589; the second, dated 1599, is *Henry V,* III.ii.28: "As young as I am I have observed these three Swashers."

[125] Some word is apparently missing here.

[126] *OED* "cut" v. 31.b. In lawn tennis, "To strike the ball sharply with the racket held at a angle, or with a downward motion, so as to make it revolve, by which it tends to shoot with a very slight rise on striking the ground." First recorded use is in 19C.

[127] *OED* "kind" n. 5.b., "in proper or good condition," i.e. properly,

or 15.b, "in repayment"? Hit back the ball with a downward motion so that it cannot be returned?

[128] *OED* "hazard": In "real tennis", "each of the winning openings in a tennis-court."

[129] *OED* "bandy" n1: "To throw or strike (a ball) to and fro, as in the game of bandy or tennis." First recorded use is 1577, in Holinshed's *Chronicles.*

[130] *OED* "chase" n. 7: "Applied to the second impact on the floor (or in a gallery) of a ball which the opponent has failed or declined to return; the value of which is determined by the nearness of the spot of impact to the end wall. If the opponent, on sides being changed, can better this stroke (i.e. cause his ball to rebound nearer the wall), he wins and scores it; if not, it is scored by the first player; until it is decided, the 'chase' is a stroke in abeyance." Making a chase is equivalent to bettering the stroke.

[131] I.e. to aim the ball at the hazard.

[132] I.e., a *bricole.* The *OED* quotes Cotgrave's definition, 1611: it is 'a side-stroake at Tennis wherein the ball goes not right forward, but hits one of the walls of the court, and thence bounds towards the [adverse] partie." It is also used figuratively. The term existed in French and Italian before it came (briefly) into English; the *OED* cites Florio, 1598, who still uses the Italian term *briccola.* (*OED* "bricole".) The first cited use of the English term, *brickwall,* dates from the same year as the publication of "The Paine of Pleasure," 1580, in Claudius Hollyband's *Treasury of the French Tongue.* (*OED* "brickwall".) See the discussion of this term in the Introduction.

[133] In the original: draws

[134] *OED* "draught": nIV.10: "The drawing of a bowshot," with a possible pun on "draft" of money.

[135] The ball used in bowling; *OED* "bowl" n2.

[136] *OED* "rub" n1

[137] A weight that makes a bowl run obliquely; the oblique path of a weighted bowl.

[138] A London expression. See *EMEDD*, Cotgrave 1611 at 28421107, 32800519.

[139] Apparently "upright bowls" is a technical term in bowling, which I have not been able to locate. Possibly bowling with pins rather than bocce-style bowling?

[140] The gutter; see *OED* "crank" n2.

[141] "Angle": a hook and line.

[142] *OED* "weel" 1, "A deep eddy"; 2, "A wicker trap for catching fish, esp. eels."

[143] *OED* "gin" n4: "A snare, net, trap or the like."

[144] *OED* "shotterel": "A young pike of the first year."

[145] See above.

[146] Frighten.

[147] A roach (a small freshwater fish like a carp).

[148] A maggot or bluebottle larva; see footnote 52.

[149] *OED* I.1: A long, narrow fishing net with floats and sinkers.

[150] In the original: mashes.

[151] The *OED* does not know the difference between this and a snipe, a woodcock (or foolish person).

[152] Sneaking, mean-spirited.

[153] *OED* 2: "A dull blockish fellow."

[154] In the original: Shoolerd. A shovelard is a spoonbill.

[155] I.e., the gun, the fowling piece.

[156] See above, footnote 151.

[157] *OED* "The pretended art of revealing future events, etc., by means of communication with the dead; more generally, magic, enchantment, conjuration."

[158] Something missing? Although this can be made into an iambic pentameter line, if somewhat awkwardly, by stressing both *heaves* and *us.*